Exile In The Promised Land

Steve Mifflin

authorHOUSE®

AuthorHouse™ UK Ltd.
500 Avebury Boulevard
Central Milton Keynes, MK9 2BE
www.authorhouse.co.uk
Phone: 08001974150

First published by AuthorHouse 7/23/2009

ISBN: 978-1-4389-9361-4 (sc)

This book is printed on acid-free paper.

The Beginning

I am undertaking a journey around England. Over the next nine months I expect to travel in excess of ten thousand miles on what I expect to be a once in a lifetime journey. An event has unexpectedly happened in my life that has generated this opportunity. On May 4th 2008, Stoke City were promoted to the Premier League for the first time after an absence of twenty three years from top flight football. No matter what happens in the future, the next nine months will be the most special period in the long history of Stoke City because a whole generation of fans will experience being in the top division of English football for the first time. It is an event unlikely to be repeated in my lifetime. Even if Stoke survive against relegation to fight another year, nothing will ever match the anticipation that is felt now.

In reality this journey started at least two generations back in my family. My dad and granddad both supported Stoke. This meant there was little option for me to buck that trend. For my generation this has meant living in the shadow of the early seventies success. It has been a painful twenty three years, but seventies Stoke fans wistfully reminiscing about Wembley and European football exacerbate the pain for those of us who measure success in terms of the Autoglass Trophy.

I am at least able to share my dad's reminiscences of the seventies during the long motorway journeys with my brother, compared to whom I am blessed. He attended his first game at the start of the 1985/6 season. Back then we all thought exclusion from the top flight would be a temporary hiccup despite the horrors of 1984/5, but the reality was things would get worse, much worse, before they got better. For me, I do at least recall Stoke playing in the old Football League Division

1, having attended my first game in 1978/9 and many games throughout the early eighties. That is of course all irrelevant history as today, Saturday August 2nd 2008, is when a new dawn breaks.

I am in Cornwall, St Ives and it is my tenth wedding anniversary. I am staying in a fabulous boutique hotel, overlooking the beach, having breakfast with Kate. Kate does not get football. Most of the time that is not necessarily a problem and in her defence she has tried. In her time she has stood on the Boothen End, she has stood on The Kop, she has been to The Brit (once) and she even saw the infamous 4-0 defeat away to Wigan at Springfield Park. She has also tried to take an interest in events unfolding earlier in the year that led to promotion. She saw Pottermouth's Battle Cry on YouTube, but her reaction to it convinced me more than ever that she is a lost cause when it comes to football. This creates problems, but it could be worse, she could support a different team and we might have to share childcare duties on match days.

Today though there is a problem, it is football related and there are still two weeks until the season starts. I sit opposite her in the hotel's breakfast room with the guilt hanging over me, wondering if she realises quite the level of football widowhood she is going to experience this season. I reach number eight in the telephone queue for Stoke City Box Office. I kind of knew for a while that the morning of our tenth wedding anniversary was at risk from the moment Stoke announced the sale of Bolton tickets to season ticket holders on that date. I knew that I was likely to be in a queue for a long time. I knew I would need to be up and ready to dial bang on 9am and I knew, despite setting expectations, this was going to be the first test of our relationship in the new Premier League world.

Frankly I am in a blind panic. I got bumped to twenty fifth in the queue despite calling bang on 9am and online there is talk of queues around The Brit of six to seven thousand people. I am also on a very dodgy mobile signal that could drop at any time. I had hoped to minimise the interruption to our romantic weekend with a quick call, tickets sorted, thanks very much, but that was never really going to happen. Instead I have been on the call for forty five minutes and am now getting lots of strange looks from the other couples in the breakfast room as Kate stares at me with my phone glued to my ear.

Breakfast arrives as I reach number two in the queue and then it is 'Hello, Stoke City Box Office,' just as I am cutting into the sausage at 10:25am. It has been nearly ninety minutes waiting, but the confirmation that there are plenty of tickets left quells my panic. Two tickets, upper tier, sorted. I return to finish my breakfast.

'We can enjoy our weekend now,' I say, but the damage is done and it is going to take some serious retail therapy on my part to put things right.

'Why couldn't your brother sort this out today?'

We both know the answer. At 11:30am I get a call from him. He has just woken up in London. 'I overslept, you sort Bolton?' he asks.

Bolton Away

1pm, Manchester Oxford Road railway station and I am glad to say it is not the South of France. There was a significant risk that I could have been watching the text version of Stoke's first ever Premier League game on a mobile phone from a foreign beach, while my kids kicked sand in my face. Last year I had already booked a two week holiday in France during the school holidays before Stoke starting flirting with the playoffs. Just knowing I would not have to miss Stoke's first game in the Premier League was a small relief that eased the pain of failing to beat QPR on the final day of the previous season. No such error this year.

Once promotion started to become a reality I countered any suggestion of foreign holidays with concern about the strength of the pound, looming recession and the virtues of holidaying in England. 'North Wales is lovely in The Summer' (and pretty close to Liverpool and Manchester) 'or what about Robin Hood's Bay?' (Newcastle, Sunderland, Middlesbrough, Hull). Now Kate knows little about football, but she is not stupid and once the fixtures were released and I started suggesting that Manchester would be a fantastic weekend break for the middle of August she smelt a rat. I had to come clean, but not before I had told my daughter all about the Lowry Centre (she has studied Lowry this year at school) and so with the combined pester power of my daughter and me, it means we are in Manchester for the weekend.

We set off from my in-laws in Oxford at 9am and a stop at Sandbach services gets me in the mood. It is mobbed with Stoke fans making the journey to Bolton. The only disappointment is that I am now going to the game as a 'Billy No Mates'. Traditionally I go to matches with my dad and brother, but my dad has opted for home games only this season, as the away games are getting a bit much for him. Also my brother had some tragic news during the week. One of his schoolmates had died in a diving accident. It is one of those shocking moments in life that puts everything else into perspective. So my brother will be at a remembrance ceremony on the day Stoke make their Premier League debut and my dad will spend the afternoon in the company of Jeff Stelling.

A member of the station staff approaches. 'Bolton train?' he asks.

'Yes, is there a problem?'

'Just got reports that it's mobbed with rowdy football fans, you might want to wait fifteen minutes and get the next one.'

'Thanks,' I say. 'Brilliant,' I think.

I love the first day of the football season and whilst it is always special, today is particularly so. The train pulls in and it is a Stoke-on-Trent party special. With many fans travelling by train from Stoke via Manchester Piccadilly, this is the connecting service to Horwich Parkway, the stop for The Reebok Stadium. There must be several hundred Stoke fans packed into a two carriage stopping service with a few bewildered looking shoppers and students wishing they had got a different train. There is no malice though as Stoke are here to party and celebrate. I am rammed in between the carriages for the journey with some other Stoke fans who boarded at Oxford Road and a couple of Greater Manchester Police, who seem torn between looking nonchalant and a bit nervous about what is going on. The banter is well meant, but even so the officers call ahead for re-enforcements to board the train at Bolton.

The atmosphere as we approach The Reebok Stadium is fantastic and with three thousand Stoke fans making the journey it is going to be a day to remember. Although one of the smaller Premier League stadiums, it is dramatic and there is a Premier League flag flying outside, which is a reminder of how far the club has come in the last few years. Inside the concourse is buzzing and you can sense the anticipation and excitement that has been building over the summer. Away days with Stoke can be intimidating, but not today. Today the atmosphere and noise is overwhelming and I have got a lump at the back of throat as the teams take to the field.

At 3pm the serious business starts. We all expect there will be more low points than high points this season, but talk of Stoke 'Doing a Derby' seems premature. All summer the press have written Stoke off as no-hopers. Even with twelve million pounds spent and more money in the transfer kitty, there is a sense from the media that Stoke City are unwelcome gatecrashers at The Premier League party. The sooner they return to The Football League the better. The hope is that Tony Pulis can turn this negative press into an incentive for the players to bond and perform. It is driving a belief amongst Stoke's fans that we should enjoy every single minute of this season even when the results are going against us. For the first half an hour of the Bolton game that is exactly what happens. Stoke look comfortable, the fans are in party mood and the only disappointment is the lack of atmosphere amongst the home supporters.

Then Bolton get lucky. Steinsson slices a cross from the by-line and it loops over Sorensen into the top corner of the goal. It is a complete fluke and Steinsson even has the decency to look half embarrassed. From that point it all goes wrong and Stoke concede two more before halftime. Stoke have fallen to pieces, there is no arguing with the 3-0 lead and the game is lost. The halftime phone calls are gloomy affairs, as the realisation dawns that Stoke probably are going to 'Do a Derby' this season. On the plus side it will be our home games that will define our destiny, but with our first four home games against sides that finished in the top seven last season, it is very realistic Stoke could have no points as Christmas approaches. With Bolton as relegation rivals, this is a game where Stoke need something.

The second half is pretty much a non-entity as Bolton coast to the win. Stoke defend well and are organised, but offer little real threat. As fulltime approaches I decide to do something I rarely do and leave early. My logic is that the game is lost so I can get an earlier train back to Manchester and meet Kate and the kids for tea. As I walk back to the station I am not alone. Suddenly there is a large cheer, which means a goal and it is immediately obvious it is Stoke who have scored. To cap a disappointing end to an historic day, I have missed Stoke's first ever Premier League goal. Still, at least I have got a wet week of camping in North Wales to look forward to.

Villa Home

After Bolton I have decided this season is not without hope. Fuller's goal was class, albeit a consolation and Stoke had performed well for large parts of the game with Kitson, Stoke's record five million pound signing, looking settled. Basically Stoke had experienced a ten minute wobble following a very lucky goal from Bolton. The bookmakers and press disagree with me. Stoke have already been written off by Paddy Power who have paid out on Stoke being relegated, even though thirty seven games remain. It is clearly a publicity stunt, but one that is offensive and it is pretty fair to say Paddy Power will get little future business from Stoke City fans. The day after the Bolton game we visited The Lowry Centre and from there you can see Old Trafford across Salford Quays. Old Trafford is a football cathedral and I consoled myself knowing that in three months Stoke would be there.

The week prior to Stoke's first Premier League home game was spent in North Wales and it did indeed rain. Now it is Saturday morning and today is the standard home game routine. Although I was born in Altrincham and spent many of my childhood weekends in and around The Potteries, I have lived in Reading for the last fifteen years and based on my accent I am now officially classed as southern. It is a three hundred mile round trip from my house to The Britannia Stadium. My home game routine involves leaving the house at 11am, getting the 11:30am train from Reading to Oxford and meeting my dad and brother at Oxford station, from where we drive two hours to The Brit. I am rarely home before 8pm on a normal match day. My brother lives in Hammersmith, which adds an extra couple of hours to his return journey.

The standard home game journey is an opportunity to catch up with family. In this respect the ritual is as much about family as it is about football. My dad is convinced Stoke would have dominated Europe for years if the roof of The Butler Street stand had not blown off and not unusually we have seventies reminiscing on the journey north. My brother is in a flap about next week's Boro away game. There are plenty of tickets left, but we had decided to give it a miss because I have a large family party at home with Kate's side of the family. My brother now wants to go to Boro, particularly because he missed Bolton. I want to go but have not put the groundwork in at home or booked advance train tickets.

Arriving at The Brit it is business as usual. The corners have not been filled in, there is no big screen scoreboard and The South Car Park is still a disgrace, despite rumours it had been sorted out. There is however a sell out crowd of twenty five thousand Stoke fans and two and half thousand Villa and once inside there is anticipation like never before. The Brit can be a desolate experience when half full, but it has found itself at last. True it has been sold out before for big games, but today it is different. Pre-match pies in a packed concourse precede taking our seats, which for this season are in the bottom tier of The John Smiths Stand. I had been a bit nervous about moving out of The Seddon Stand because The John Smith's lacks atmosphere, but my dad's health means he needs to be close to the car park so the move was necessary. I should not have worried, all sides of the stadium are rocking and the Villa fans are up for it as well. There has never been a pre-match atmosphere like this before.

Any thoughts of an anti-climatic Stoke performance are erased as soon as the teams kick off. Stoke are straight in at Villa from the off and Rory Delap is firing in the long throws. To a large extent I have always felt the Delap throw, whilst spectacular, is somewhat ineffective. Today though, Villa look rattled early on as Stoke press them. The first half hour sees a

9

few decent chances for Stoke, but on the occasions Villa break, they look dangerous. On thirty minutes the first major drama unfolds as Fuller is felled in the box. It looks like a penalty and there is a huge shout and appeal from Stoke. There is no serious doubt, the penalty is given and Lawrence steps up. This might not be Stoke's first Premier League goal, but it is the first one that actually matters. Lawrence dispatches it brilliantly and peels away in front of the John Smiths's stand like a man possessed, palming the Premier League badge on his arm. This matters so much and there is bedlam all around. Stoke have arrived.

Villa are fancied to do well in The Premier League this year, but Stoke go in at halftime beating them at home and deservedly so. It is one of those classic games where you do not want halftime to come. So often Stoke will sit back and try to defend 1-0 so we expect more of the same today and against a class Villa strike force it could be fatal. Often it is effective, but it is also nerve wracking to watch. There are chances at either end, but a slick move by Villa brings the scores level on the hour. 'I'll take the point now off the back of a good performance. Just don't lose the game Stoke.'

It is tense stuff, but with just ten minutes left in the game Fuller is clear through after an exquisite little flick and turn that catches the Villa defence cold. It is perfection, but the angle is tight and Fuller often pulls shots after making these sorts of chances. Everyone is up on their feet, but today is not the day for fluffed lines. The ball is hammered across goal just inside the far post and words cannot describe what happens. Not only has Fuller just scored one of the best goals seen at the Brit, but it is one of the most important. He has probably just won the game with a wonder goal. Never have I seen scenes at a Stoke home game like those that followed Fuller's goal. I am hugging strangers and holding back tears.

Any tension about holding on for the win is short lived though. Villa create a well-worked equaliser as the stewards continue to sort out the aftermath of Fuller's goal. It is cruel and the Villa fans know it. Now they are up and loving it, goading the Premier League new boys. There is only one thought in my mind, 'Do not throw this away Stoke. It would be unbearable. We deserve our first point in The Premier League.' That said, Villa also seem happy with a point. It is likely we will go home satisfied, but thinking about what might have been. Deep into injury time the ball goes out on the far side and Delap steps up. His throws have caused problems today, so there is one last chance. He fires it in, there is contact, The Boothen End are on their feet and the ball loops agonisingly over the bar. 'How good would that have been?'

Four minutes of injury time played and people are leaving. The ball goes out of play directly in front of us. Delap will get another chance and everyone is on their feet chanting his name. He fires it in, this time Sidibe rises and makes contact. It is right in front of me, perfectly in line and I know the ball is going to loop in the top corner long before it hits the back of the net. The Boothen End goes up to confirm it. In my time I have celebrated many disallowed goals and often been one of the last to realise when a goal has been ruled out. So nowadays I will usually double check that the goal has been given before letting myself go. Not today though, this was somehow destined to happen and this is our moment. I am lost in my own world before the ball has even hit the back of the net. To be totally lost in a goal celebration is a rare thing. I am pretty sure I did not cry, but it was a close thing. By the time I know what is going on, the game has finished and the taunting of the few remaining Villa fans is in full swing. With all four sides of the ground up and chanting, it must have been an intimidating sight as an away fan. No away fan will ever admit that of course, but I would challenge any Villa fan to disagree that they too had witnessed something pretty special today.

After the game I am totally drained and without much discussion we are at the box office to get tickets for Cheltenham and Middlesbrough. Back in The South Car Park it is joyous.

My dad seems fighting fit, which after what has just been experienced is a blessing. These days he usually greets the goals with casual applause from his seat, but I caught a glimpse of him after the winning goal and he was up there with the rest of them.

Cheltenham Away

There are three things I will never tire of watching after the Villa game: Fuller's goal, The Boothen End after Sidibe's winner and the reaction to the closing moments of the game on Soccer Saturday. The video of Phil Thompson has been doing the rounds on YouTube and I love it. The media attention has been huge following the Villa win. It was the featured game on Match Of The Day, Tony Pulis was in the studio for a Match Of The Day 2 special feature and I spent Sunday reading every sports supplement I could get my hands on. The Brit atmosphere and Delap long throw are attracting attention. There is even a suggestion Stoke are not now certain relegation candidates. Maybe, maybe not, but I am now convinced Stoke will not 'Do a Derby'. After all Stoke have now equalled Derby's total win tally last season after just the second game.

I broke the news to Kate about Boro away. Given the family party situation on Saturday, she has taken this remarkably well. I have a suspicion that she might have realised it will be difficult to keep Jeff Stelling from crashing the party and with Kate's family predominantly egg chasers, Jeff is not a welcome guest. Maybe she is thinking it is best if I am not there, because even if I am in Reading in person, mentally I will be at The Riverside Stadium anyway. Whatever the reason she has given it her blessing and despite my guilt at bombing out the family party I am in no mood to miss the trip to Teesside.

Tonight should be a good night. No Premier League pressure and a small Stoke following to a new ground that is fairly local for me. I love small, away, evening games where you get the Stoke hardcore plus a few exiles. My dad has a mate Steve, who is a Cheltenham Town season ticket holder, so he has been to a few games with him at Whaddon Road. Tonight he will be sitting with the Cheltenham fans rather than with Stoke, so it is another away game on my own, as my brother has not made the trip from London. I meet my dad at Oxford station after leaving work early and we drive to Eynsham where we meet Steve and his nine year old nephew, Paul. We drive to Cheltenham in Steve's battered Astra and I am in the back with Paul. He is a nice kid with a good knowledge of football and games consoles. It is not the worst journey I have ever had to football, but it is a bit different from the usual away games with my brother. Having exhausted Xbox experiences and our shared knowledge of football, which given the age difference has not taken too long, I turn to a question that has been troubling me. 'Why are you wearing a Chelsea shirt to a Cheltenham game?'

'Well last year I supported Arsenal, but now I support Chelsea.'

'Oh', it is not quite the answer I was expecting. I wonder what kind of reaction taking a kid into The Boothen End wearing a Man United shirt might cause.

Whaddon Road is a great little ground and whilst I had not put too much thought into this League Cup distraction, it is of course a big game for Cheltenham now that Stoke have Premier League status. We drop the car at Steve's dad's, which is about thirty yards from the ground. Steve's dad is over ninety and before I know it I am in the social club enjoying a couple of pre-match pints with Steve's family and friends. Steve's dad starts recounting tales of Stanley Matthews. It is a very relaxed atmosphere and there are a few Stoke faces I recognise as hard core enjoying Cheltenham Town's warm welcome.

I guess part of the reason for the relaxed atmosphere is that this game does not really matter. In years gone by it annoyed me when the big Premier League teams started disrespecting the cup competitions, but now it is the norm and common even amongst The Championship sides. You have to fear for the future of our domestic cup competitions, but for the first time I fully appreciate the sentiment that means it will be Stoke reserves playing Cheltenham tonight in this League Cup second round match.

I have got a ticket on row E, so near the front, but when I get inside I realise row E is one row from the back of the away stand. There will be no smaller ground than this visited this season. It is another 3-2 win to Stoke and one that could not be more different from the Villa game. Three games down, seven goals scored and seven conceded. Have we seen the end of Stoke City binary football? Despite the suggestion that the game is close it is not really. The highlights are a sweet free kick from Whelan, a second from Cresswell and an over the top goal celebration from Parkin after what is, to be fair, a great finish for the third.

Although I want to avoid any arrogance as a Premier League new boy, it is difficult not to have a sense that Stoke have just dispatched a lesser team with ease. Even so, we should not forget that it is only six years since visits to grounds like Whaddon Road were commonplace. After the game Steve's dad seems more concerned about having been sat too close to the guy with the drum, than the fact that Cheltenham have been ejected from The League Cup. I try and recall the last time Stoke were in the League Cup third round. It was probably in the seventies.

Middlesbrough Away

The run up to the first full Premier League away day with my brother has not gone smoothly, as we have missed all the cheap train tickets. With the prospect of a six hundred mile round trip ahead, the only realistic options are the train or flights. With flying to Teesside excessively expensive at such short notice, I have had to spend over a hundred quid on a walk on fare from Reading to Middlesbrough. Although the match tickets are not expensive by Premier League standards, this is the real start of the eye watering expense that we are going to incur this season following Stoke.

As a result of the train fares, we are in a bit of 'in for a penny, in for a pound' frame of mind and determined to enjoy every minute of the day regardless of the score. Beers are sunk on the two and half hour trip from London Kings Cross to Darlington in what is a fairly uneventful journey. The train is packed, but for a Saturday, surprisingly devoid of football fans.

Having arrived at Darlington around 2pm expecting to find the station mobbed with Boro and Stoke fans getting the connection to Middlesbrough, it is disappointing to find the station pretty much deserted. Darlington provides the opportunity to top up the beer and when the connection pulls in I am hoping it will be full of Stoke's train travelling fans providing some pre-match atmosphere. No such luck, the train is so empty I am suddenly hit by a wave of paranoia that the game is off.

Middlesbrough recently stole the crown from Stoke-on-Trent as the worst place to live in Britain. There is little to suggest, as the train pulls into Middlesbrough station, that the award is not fully deserved, but the friendliness of the Boro fans who have boarded at the intermediate stations is testament to the hospitality of the North East. It has also allayed any paranoia about the game being called off.

The approach to The Riverside Stadium on foot is similar to that of The Brit from the Trentham End, but even more desolate. The Riverside is now fully enclosed and is a dramatic landmark amongst the wasteland. Stoke have not sold their full ticket allocation, but it is still a huge following and with the away end on a single tier the pre-match atmosphere in the concourse is buzzing. By the time we have consumed a couple of pie & pint combos I am more than ready for a lager fuelled ninety minutes of singing.

Having made the effort to get there, I am probably a bit too boozed up to fully appreciate the game, but a number of things stick in my mind about the first half. Firstly the Stoke fans are well up for it, secondly the Stoke players are well up for it, and thirdly the referee has robbed Stoke of any chance of getting something out of this game after unjustly sending off Amdy Faye when he clearly got the ball. With Alves scoring from the resulting free kick, there is no way back against a dangerous looking Boro attack when Stoke have only got ten men. I am cursing the injustice of the situation at halftime along with every other Stoke fan. It seems everyone saw Amdy Faye get the ball and this is just a typical example of how The Premier League looks after the established clubs, at the cost to any newcomers.

A lack of communication with my brother means that we both buy halftime rounds, so it is going to be a struggle to get two pints down in the fifteen minute break. The screens in the concourse show the first half highlights and there is a hush as the Faye incident replays. There is a discernable intake of breath. Faye may have got the ball, but he did it two footed at knee height. It is ugly and the referee has got the decision right. The cursing of the referee has been replaced by genuine fear that Stoke will get stuffed in the second half as we return upstairs. The Stoke fans are all stood pretty much anywhere for this game so we move to seats right in the middle behind the goal.

The halftime beers kick in and with the game seemingly lost it is a party atmosphere anyway. Everyone is standing, everyone is singing and the guy next to me is still berating the referee. 'Mate, check it out on Match Of The Day tonight', I tell him, 'I've just seen it on the screens downstairs.'

'Why? Was it bad?'

'Just a bit.' He joins the party mood after that.

Stoke defend well, but create little and then a penalty is conceded. Downing steps up and cracks the ball against the bar much to the delight of the Stoke fans. The volume cranks up a notch. The home crowd has been virtually silent all game and although the atmosphere in the away end is as good as I have seen it at a Stoke game, the overall atmosphere at The Riverside is disappointing. Stoke have ridden their luck, stood firm with ten men and with Boro failing to kill the game off, Stoke get a break with twenty minutes left. Lawrence puts in a wicked cross and Hoyle, under pressure from Kitson, fails to deal with it. An own goal, against the run of play, sends all of us delirious. I am grabbed and hugged by the guy next to me. Stoke just need to hang on for a valuable away point.

It does not happen. Late into the game Boro get a winner. It is not the kind of injury time goal that will leave you sick and in truth a Boro win is a fair result. Stoke battle for the last five minutes, but Boro hold out. When all is said and done I leave The Riverside reasonably happy, particularly with the commitment of the players and the passion of the Stoke following. My brother and I both agree it has been worth the trip and on the walk back to the station we chat with Boro fans about their aspirations for the season. Everyone we speak to seems pleased to see Stoke back in the top division.

Back at the station there is time for a couple of pints in one of the bars before we have to catch our train. The atmosphere is genuinely friendly and there seems to be no issue with Stoke and Boro fans mixing it up in the local pubs. We have got reservations back to London via York and it is the York train that the Stoke fans are also using. There is a large number travelling back across the Pennines by train and the general consensus is that with Boro expected to do well this season, we can take a lot of heart from this particular away performance. On a different day we might even have come away with a point. A few Stoke and Boro fans make the connection to London at York. For my brother and I we have now been on the beers for eight hours and with the heat of day and adrenalin of the match we are both starting to flag.

The train from York to London is non-stop, but will still take a couple of hours. There is not enough time to buy more beer on the station and when we get on board the train the buffet car is sold out. We get on the shorts and after that it is all a little bit vague. I clearly recall having a sing-off with some Posh fans at Peterborough station out of the train window, I vaguely recall singing Deliah at Kings Cross station, but I have pretty much no recollection of getting home.

Everton Home

Stoke have got the early kick off on Super Sunday for what will be one of the biggest home games of the year. Everton have been knocking on the door of 'The Big Four' in recent seasons, but have had a slow start and after three games, are in the relegation zone. Stoke are above them by just one goal. This will be a tough game, but with another full house at The Brit, if Stoke can show the passion on and off the pitch it is not without hope.

There has been a two week break since the last game because of internationals. Many have said that having a break so early in the season is a bad thing, but after the Boro away game, for me personally it could not have come soon enough. To say I was in the doghouse on the Sunday after Boro would be a massive understatement. On the football free weekend we had planned a camping trip with family friends, but with storms forecast, we had gone away to Birmingham instead and visited Cadbury World. Even with no football, I had not fully managed to be completely Stoke City free as much of Saturday morning was spent securing tickets for Liverpool away during a break in the journey on the M42. Getting tickets for our first 'Big Four' away game was always going to be stressful, as demand would far exceed supply. However having attended Bolton, Cheltenham and Boro, I was now on the priority list for Liverpool away.

Back to today though and I have driven from Reading to Stoke, picking my dad up on the way. Sunday train services do not lend themselves well to early kick offs. My brother is on a stag do in South Wales. He knew immediately the fixtures were announced that he probably would not be able to attend the Everton or Chelsea home games due to stag do and wedding commitments. Pre-match, the atmosphere is not quite as up as the Villa game. With an early kick off things are often a bit muted, but once the teams emerge the noise levels rise.

It rises even more on the first Delap long throw, as it is obvious Everton, like Villa, are going to struggle to deal with it. The first twenty minutes is all Stoke, but Everton start to show some class and turn the game around. There is little arguing when Everton take the lead on forty minutes following a Sorenson blunder by the corner flag. It is disappointing, but there is enough to suggest Stoke can still get something from this game. That hope is short lived when Everton score a second straight after halftime. Soft goals either side of halftime have exposed Stoke's defence and shown Everton to be a class team. 'This is going to end up five or six', my dad says. I fear he could be right.

We are both wrong. Everton's defence fail to deal with Stoke pressure and almost immediately Stoke are back in it. The goal is a cracking volley from Olofinjana right in front of The Boothen End. The noise is deafening and all of a sudden Everton look like they are wobbling. Just minutes later Fuller wins the ball brilliantly from Yobo, rounds the keeper and slots home the equaliser. This sparks delirious celebrations again and it takes a very long time for everyone, including Fuller himself, to realise the goal has been disallowed. It seems genuinely unjust. Yobo went down under a challenge from Fuller that seemed fair. The full venom of The Boothen End is unleashed on the referee and for once it is justified.

The rollercoaster of emotion this generates is the perfect precursor to what happens next. The ball goes out of play and Delap steps up. Everyone is up on their feet and The Boothen End is willing the ball in. Delap fires and there is total panic in the Everton defence. Bodies are pushed all over the place and the ball deflects into the back of the net. It looks ugly and there has to be a case for a foul, but the referee is going to have to be a very brave man to disallow two in two minutes, especially when the first was so controversial. My immediate reaction is that Howard has flapped and punched it in his own net. The reaction of the Stoke players certainly suggests it is an own goal. Replays will show Jagielka to be the culprit. Who cares? It is in, Stoke are level and there is still half an hour to win the game. If Stoke can get the winner now, this will be bigger than the Villa win.

I feel sure Stoke will now win the game, but Everton are not settling for a draw. You can spend years following football and rarely witness this kind of drama. With emotions running high Cort handles inside the box and it looks like an obvious penalty from where I am. There follows a long discussion around the incident and it is unclear what is going on. The referee seems to have lost control of the game, but it has to be a penalty to Everton or a free kick to Stoke for the push on Cort. The decision to award a free kick to Everton outside the box stuns everyone and clearly delights the Stoke fans. It is too much for Moyes who gets sent from the dug out, but with the tunnel in the corner at The Brit, Moyes has to sit behind the dug out with the Stoke fans. You could not script this if you were making it up.

The final piece of drama comes ten minutes from time and is a well worked corner from Everton that is poorly defended by Stoke. Cahill fires home the header and celebrates in front of the Everton fans. Cahill has not played for Everton for months and you can see what this means to Everton and their fans. It is a huge goal and a huge celebration on the away end. Stoke have chances and a penalty shout in the final ten minutes, but today is Everton's day. It is rare that I leave the ground following a Stoke defeat not disappointed, but today was a day that gives us huge hope for the season ahead. You can honestly say we got value for money for the entertainment on show.

Liverpool Away

Stoke have got the Scousers two weeks in a row and this is without doubt one of the most highly anticipated games of the season. Getting tickets has not been without controversy, but both my brother and I have managed to get them. With the Everton game there was no Scouse interaction, but today will be different. Scouse Phil and his family are meeting us off the train at Lime Street. Scouse Phil is my brother's old flatmate. He is from Aintree, but lives in London and goes to every home and away game including all Liverpool's European matches. He has also just lost his job in the banking crisis.

Transport for this game has turned into a total nightmare as our pre-booked trains have been cancelled due to engineering works. The main line from Crewe to Liverpool is closed all weekend. This means changing train tickets at the last minute to get us into Liverpool early enough and then having to book a flight home from Manchester. Before I set foot outside the door at 7:20am, the day has already cost me nearly two hundred quid. My 7:40am Reading departure is timed to meet with my brother's 8:10am London departure at Birmingham New Street. I have serious doubts that he will have made his train if his usual Friday night has run to form.

I join him for the journey from Birmingham to Stockport. Stockport station is full of Stoke fans, but there are also hundreds of other travellers struggling with the line closures. Our reserved seats do not exist when the train pulls in. It seems the service has been borrowed from an old siding in East Anglia and with the temperature outside already well above twenty degrees, having the heating on full seems a little unnecessary. Just as things seem like they cannot get worse the train pulls into Manchester Piccadilly and it is total chaos. Travelling in style this is not.

A large contingent of Merseyside Police meets the train at Lime Street. Given the only trouble I have witnessed so far this season has been a bit of handbags on Bolton station, it all seems a little heavy handed, but I guess we have to concede that Stoke fans have made their bed over the last twenty years and this is the price we have to pay. Scouse Phil seems very excited when we meet him. 'We've got the special forces out for your lot today, so no thieving while you're up here alright?'

'Don't worry we've brought the super heroes with us today, can't take any chances up here' is the reply. Secretly I am a bit gutted he has put one over on us with a thieving gag before we have even shaken hands. Batman, Robin, Banana Man and a well-endowed Wonder Woman follow us through the ticket barrier.

We are whisked away to a nearby pub. As well as Scouse Phil, there is Scouse Phil's dad, Scouse Phil's brother and Scouse Phil's brother's bird (she does not seem too unhappy with the given label) plus a lot of other Scousers, all of whom could well be related to Phil. I appear to be given the honour of the chair in the pub and initially feel a bit distressed about the size of the round until I get charged five pounds forty for six pints. 'Happy hour, welcome to Liverpool'.

There then follows two hours of drinking and plenty of reminiscing about Liverpool's games in The Potteries, not least Liverpool's last visit, when Stoke suffered a humiliating 8-0 defeat. It is good, well meant banter, but there is a strong air of confidence that 8-0 might not be unrealistic again today. There is also a strong belief that this will be Liverpool's year, with Liverpool having beaten Man United the previous week and currently sharing top spot with Chelsea. On the cab ride to Anfield, Scouse Phil's brother tells a story of how he mistook a hand dryer for a urinal in a Lisbon café when travelling away with Liverpool to a Sporting Lisbon game. He is not disappointing us as a Scouse stereotype.

We arrive at a pub somewhere behind The Kop and it is packed. There is not a Stoke fan in sight and it is slightly intimidating as I head for the bar now that my round is up again. Scouse Phil's brother pulls me back with an incredulous look on his face. He is either going to front the round or he has just saved me from being beaten to a pulp. It turns out it is neither scenario and next thing I know we are in the off-licence next door negotiating a bulk buy on cans. We return to the pub car park and join the masses, the majority of whom also seem to be drinking cans from the off-licence. When we got promoted I had visions of arriving at places like Anfield with hours to spare, seeing the Shankly Gates and getting inside with an hour to kill as the Stoke boys build up the atmosphere. In reality, at 2:50pm we are still in the pub and we are arguing about flags. Apparently it is a day for 'Cracking the flags', but as I have no idea what they are talking about I just nod, drain my can and look at my watch.

Scouse Phil apologises that Liverpool Football Club may not have had chance to disinfect the away seats following the visit of the 'Dirty Mancs' and we go our separate ways on The Anfield Road. We are in our seats at 2:58pm and at 3:02pm Stoke are 1-0 down. A Gerrard free kick has flown in the top corner to the stunned disbelief of the large and noisy Stoke following. I spend the next few minutes in a heat and booze induced state of confusion while half the Stoke fans are back up and getting behind the team and the other half are just stunned. The scoreboard still says 0-0 and I have to confirm with my brother that the Gerrard goal has actually been disallowed even though the game has been underway again for several minutes. He does not seem to know what is going on either and it is obvious that many around us are thinking the same. It becomes apparent that it is a huge let off for Stoke as Gerrard's goal looked to be good. Liverpool lay siege and Stoke defend deep. Miraculously Stoke reach halftime and it is still 0-0 with the only real chance falling to Kitson, who put his shot over the bar.

With no beer on sale at halftime, we stay in our seats and with the heat, beer and tension of the game taking its toll I sit down for the first time and suddenly feel the fatigue hitting me. My phone rings and it is my dad calling for the halftime report. 'I've just seen you on TV,' he says, 'you both look terrible, what have you been doing?' He knows full well, so I do not provide him the satisfaction of telling him we have been on the beers since 11am. He finishes the call by telling me Stoke will get stuffed and I fear he could be right.

The second half is more of the same and it is only a matter of time before Liverpool score. Stoke defend in numbers and all the back players perform heroics. At seventy five minutes and with the score still 0-0, there is the first sense that Stoke might get something from the game. Every Stoke challenge and every Liverpool miss is greeted with huge cheers. The Liverpool fans, who have stood in silent disbelief since Gerrard's ruled out goal, are starting to leave. We enter the last five minutes as chance after chance goes begging for Liverpool. A winner for Liverpool is still expected, but it would be cruel now. Ninety minutes on the clock and three minutes of added time are shown. It is the longest three minutes ever and I can barely watch. When the referee blows the celebrations are wild. Stoke fans have never celebrated a 0-0 draw this much, well except maybe when Stoke drew 0-0 with Leicester last season to clinch promotion. Stoke's first ever Premier League away point could not have come at a better time or better place. The Kop has been out sung and Stoke have seriously dented Liverpool's Championship aspirations.

Outside I am drained as I leave my brother. He is staying over in Liverpool and I need to get back to Lime Street. I walk through Anfield alone trying to get a cab and a big Scouse lad walks over shaking his head, 'Nightmare, what a nightmare'.

I could have just nodded and agreed, but I say 'Depends on who you support'.

'That's all I need is some blue nose to rub it in.'

'No, I'm Stoke', I correct him, suddenly wondering if this is a very stupid situation to have got myself into.

He looks at me, hesitates then raises his arm. Just as I am thinking this could be very bad, his arm goes around my shoulder. 'Your boys have got some fight. You're going to be fine this season. Good to see Stoke back. All the best.' It is a touching statement to complete the day and I am still smiling five and half hours later when I get home. It is perfect timing for Match Of The Day, but when Kate answers the door I know that I will have to wait until Sunday morning for that. Still at least the journey home has sobered me up and it is no repeat of the Boro away game.

Reading Home

Stoke have drawn my local team in the League Cup third round. Reading are fancied to be promoted straight back to The Premier League after being relegated on the last day of the season on goal difference. This means Reading are about as interested in a League Cup run as Stoke are. It is going to be Stoke reserves against Reading reserves for a place in the last sixteen. Had the game been at The Madejski Stadium I would have gone, but am I going to do the three hundred mile round trip to watch a meaningless midweek cup-tie? No. Call me a glory hunter if you like, but 'Stoke City Fan' and 'Glory Hunter' is a contradiction in terms, even this season.

So for the first time this season I am settled on my sofa to spend two hours in front of Sky Sports with my laptop while Stoke are playing. In the end it is quite a bit more than two hours in what turns out to be quite a remarkable game. Firstly Pericard scores. I did not even realise he was still at the club, but with Parkin now sold and our other strikers rested, he gets the nod from Pulis. Then the game goes to penalties when it is 2-2 after extra time and remarkably Stoke win with Pericard scoring the winning penalty. Have Stoke ever won a penalty shoot out? Stoke in the last sixteen of the League Cup. Maybe it is time to start taking an interest.

Chelsea Home

My mum and dad are visiting my auntie and uncle in Clayton. My brother is at a wedding. I have planned ahead and got a cheap train ticket from Reading to Stoke and will be picked up from Stoke station by my dad. Inexplicably first class is cheaper than standard class, so it is a bit of luxury for the journey. On departing from Reading at 9:40am I sit next to an Exeter City (initially mistaken as a Southampton) fan travelling up to Macclesfield Town. Most Chelsea fans will travel up direct from London and with the train due into Stoke at 1:20pm, it is a bit early for any Chelsea or Stoke fans to join this train. Once I have bored the Exeter fan with tales of the Premier League, I relax and read the papers. It feels like Stoke have started well in The Premier League, but in reality four points from five games sees them in the relegation zone. Stoke's relegation rivals have started stronger, particularly Hull who are grabbing the early headlines. Looking at the teams for today, it seems without hope that Stoke can get something from this game given Chelsea's spending power. I manage to watch the League Cup fourth round draw on Soccer AM as I change trains at Birmingham New Street. Stoke draw Rotherham at home. It is a great opportunity to progress into the quarterfinals, but being a Stoke fan I know this is crazy talk.

On arrival at Stoke station there is a big police operation in progress, but with it still being early, most of them are standing around looking bored. There are a few Chelsea shirts and a couple of Stoke shirts on show. My dad picks me up and my mum and auntie are in the car. They drop us at the ground on their way to Trentham Gardens. As a result we end up outside The Brit at half past one just as the Chelsea team coach turns up. It might be early, but there is a hostile welcome for The Premier League rich boys as they get off their coach.

Another sell-out and another spine tingling atmosphere greets the players. The Chelsea boys are well up for it as well, which adds to the pre-match noise. The atmosphere at all of Stoke's games this season has to be witnessed first hand to be believed and again today it is no exception. The team sheets reflect the gulf between Stoke and Chelsea with every one of Chelsea's team a household name, Cech, Terry, Cole, Lampard, Ballack, Drogba and today Chelsea's new sixteen million pound signing Bosingwa is also playing. Chelsea's side has cost well in excess of one hundred million to assemble and although Stoke have spent large by their standards, about twelve million, it is men against boys today in terms of the finances available. Scolari has had his team focussed on defending the Delap long throw, such has been the media interest in Stoke's unusual attacking weapon, but today Delap is injured so he need not have bothered.

Stoke, roared on by a passionate home crowd, equip themselves well, but there is little sense of an upset on the cards as Chelsea deal with everything thrown at them. Arguably Stoke show Chelsea too much respect. Some half chances fall to Chelsea, but Stoke's back line deal with them. Sorenson and Abdoulaye Faye stand out. It is starting to become clear that Stoke carried out some excellent business over the summer with those signings. On thirty six minutes a neat Chelsea move sees Bosingwa break clear and fire into the far corner from a difficult angle. The referee misses the initial handball, but it is still a class finish by a class player and there is not much arguing with the 1-0 halftime score.

Kitson, who is still yet to fire this season, is replaced by Fuller early in the second half and Fuller looks well up for it. It changes the game as Fuller causes problems for the Chelsea defence. Stoke win corners and free kicks and Chelsea look threatening on the counter attack. On about sixty minutes there is a huge goalmouth scramble and a great chance falls to Sidibe, but it is cleared off the line. Just when it begins to feel like Stoke can get something from the game, a vital slip by Cort allows Anelka to score and it finishes Stoke off. The game is lost, but Stoke have not been humiliated and have given Chelsea a bit of a scare on the way.

I leave right on the final whistle and head for the canal to walk back to the station. With my seat right by the exit and with a brisk walk, by the time I get to City Road I am pretty much alone and looking forward to a pint in The Roebuck before getting the train at 6:10pm. When I get to Glebe Street I am surprised to see The Roebuck boarded up. In truth I have not been there since Ipswich at home last season, so it could have been shut down for six months for all I know. The second surprise is getting stopped by the police. 'Sorry, you can't go any further', I am told.

'What do mean? I need to get a train at 6pm.'. The constable blocking the road appears baffled by this.

'OK, but cover your colours and go in the North Stafford until it is time for your train.'

This all seems ridiculous, but having a drink in The North Stafford is fine so I oblige and make my way down Station Road. As I approach the station coach after coach of Chelsea fans arrive at the station and the police try and herd them onto the awaiting football special. Chelsea's fans are more intent on trying to get into the hotel for a swift one before the train departs than following any of the police directions. It now makes sense why the police are trying to keep Stoke fans away from the station. In the North Staffs I head to the back bar and there are about twenty or so Chelsea fans drinking. This suddenly feels a bit intimidating for a home game. Usually there are plenty of Stoke fans getting trains after home games, but not today.

Once the Chelsea football special departs and the station is opened, I head over to wait for the Reading train. There are now plenty of Stoke fans, but still loads of Chelsea fans boarding my train south. A healthy police presence joins the train as well. I am quite happy to find my seat in first class and I end up sitting next to a guy in Chelsea colours who introduces himself as John. John is travelling down to Basingstoke. He explains that there has been a frantic effort to ensure no Chelsea fans board the scheduled service to London at 6:30pm, because that is the train from Manchester and Man United have been playing at home. Allowing Chelsea to travel on the same train as the Cockney Reds is a potential tinderbox for trouble.

Chelsea John suggests we head for the buffet, but with the train packed I recommend we wait until after Stafford where most Stoke fans will depart. Even after Stafford the train is still rammed with a lot of Chelsea, a lot of Exeter City and a few Stoke fans. On the way down the train we meet a Stoke fan on crutches propped in the doorway who Chelsea John seems to know. He introduces me to Dave from Brighton. It is unclear how Chelsea John and Brighton Dave know each other, but Chelsea John tells Brighton Dave to get himself up to first class. The buffet car is sold out of lager so we hit the red wine. Back in first class Chelsea John pays for Brighton Dave's upgrade. It is a nice touch. It turns out that despite having MS, Brighton Dave regularly drives from Brighton to Reading to get the train to Stoke's home games. It is unbelievable commitment.

After Birmingham, the train empties out a bit with a large number of Chelsea fans making the connection back to London. Chelsea John heads back to the buffet car. He returns with more wine. Drinking heavily on this journey was not my intention, but now it is inevitable. I feel obliged to return the round and just after Banbury I make my way down the train to the buffet car with full colours showing. I get grabbed on the way down, but there is no malice, it is the Exeter City fan I met on the way up. 'Alright mate?'

'Yeah, you had a good day?'

'Yep, won 4-1, not so good for you though.'

'No, but no real expectations against Chelsea.'

'Meet some new friends of mine,' and I am introduced to some Chelsea lads. There is a bit of banter about the game and then I am told something truly shocking. Hull City have beaten Arsenal at The Emirates in the late kick off. The Chelsea boys are obviously delighted, but frankly I am getting sick of Hull taking all the new boy praise instead of Stoke. I continue my journey to the buffet car and I get 'Stokie, give us song, Stokie, Stokie give us song' as I make my way down the carriage. In the buffet car there are a couple of Stoke lads travelling to Oxford and we agree to give a bit of Delilah back to them. I return to Chelsea John and Brighton Dave with 'One song, you've only got one song' ringing in my ears.

The train gets to Reading at 8:40pm and bolstered by the drink I stroll through Reading station with full colours on display. Swansea City are in town and have been thumped 4-0 by Reading. The Swansea boys should be long gone, but there are a few stragglers. I hear 'Oi, nob head, what are you doing here?' and it is clearly a Welsh accent. I don't run, but I do not look back either and dive into the nearest cab and home. It has been a great day out and I am not keen to have it spoiled by getting a pasting on Reading station. In the cab I try and sober up a bit, but as I get in the house one look from Kate and I know it is a lost cause. I do not even make it past 9pm before I am crashed out.

Portsmouth Away

Simonsen makes his first Premier League start and following a bizarre injury to Lawrence involving his dog, new signing Tongue makes his full Stoke debut. One person not at Fratton Park though is me. For nearly a year Kate and I had a weekend away in Newcastle planned for The Great North Run. When the fixtures were announced I had hoped to get one of the North East teams away. So when Portsmouth came up, unless the game got moved to Monday I was not going to be able to attend. A bit surprisingly, given Portsmouth's close proximity to London and Oxford, neither my dad nor my brother attends either. My dad is on holiday and Sunday engineering works make it virtually impossible for my brother to attend by train. In truth it is a blessing that Stoke are not also in the North East this weekend, as I have been clearly pushing my luck with Kate and this is the chance to spend some quality time together before the hectic November fixtures really kick in.

We arrived in Newcastle on Friday night and awoke to find Arsenal staying in the hotel prior to their away game at Sunderland. When the lift doors open after breakfast there is stood Almunia, Denilson and Fabregas. I am half expecting Kate to go all star struck, but she nonchalantly steps into the lift. I do the same, but I suspect I am a bit less nonchalant as I nod to our fellow lift passengers. Denilson gives a knowing smile and I imagine they must enjoy seeing the reaction of people in situations like this. We exit the lift and I say to Kate, 'Did you recognise them?'

'Who?'

'Almunia, Denilson and Fabregas.'

'Who?'

'You must have heard of Fabregas.'

'Yeah, alright', she says getting narky. I let it drop, but later that evening she is on the phone to her sister. 'Who was that footballer we saw today?' Kate asks me. Her sister is about to marry a Gooner.

'Fabregas.' There is an audible scream down the phone.

'No way, you were in the same lift as Cesc Fabregas?' I hear her scream. Kate knowing absolutely nothing about football does have its advantages in situations like this morning. At least there was no embarrassing autograph chasing, give us a kiss, can I have a photo moment. Kate is a classy girl and I often wonder what she ever saw in me.

So it is now Sunday afternoon and I have managed to get away to the bar to experience the game via Sky Sports News and BBC online on my phone. Obviously it is disappointing to miss my first game of the season, but I have been to Portsmouth loads of times and their away end is a total disgrace. Ultimately Stoke lose the game through a spectacular Crouch goal and Defoe winner. This is after Stoke have drawn level from a Fuller goal created from a Delap long throw. The Delap long throw is becoming legendary. I guess there were no big expectations from Portsmouth away, but four points from seven games is starting to feel perilous.

Tottenham Home

Given Spurs have been knocking on the door of 'The Big Four' in recent seasons, this game would not have been targeted as a 'must win' game at the start of the season. However with Stoke on just four points and placed nineteenth in the league, they are getting desperate for a win. Spurs' start to the season has been the big talking point. It has been a disaster and they are bottom of the table on just two points, their worst ever start to a Premier League season. This has placed Ramos under huge pressure and he is now odds-on to be the first Premier League manager to be sacked this season. Keegan has already departed from Newcastle and Curbishley from West Ham, but those were resignations. We still await the first Premier League sacking.

This game is taking centre stage on Sky Sports flagship Super Sunday programme as the 4pm kick off and it has been billed by Sky as the first big relegation six pointer of the season. In reality, it is too early to be talking of relegation six pointers and in the full knowledge that Spurs have some world class players, concern that they are bound to click at some point counters the genuine belief that Stoke can win this game. No one really believes Spurs will actually get relegated. This morning my brother came over to Reading from London and because of engineering works we got picked up by my dad from Didcot rather than Oxford. It is the first time the three of us have all been to a game together since Villa at home.

Inside The Brit, the atmosphere is unbelievable again. The Stoke fans want to put Stoke-on-Trent on the map in front of Sky's global audience. The Brit has also been officially recognised as the nosiest stadium in England following research carried out by Sky Sports. It is building a reputation as the stadium that teams do not want to visit because of the robust and direct tactics employed by Pulis and the hostility of the home supporters. With the Tottenham fans up for it today and Stoke fans already goading Ramos, the pre-match atmosphere is as good as it has been for our other home games. I text three friends who support Tottenham and who I know will be watching the game on TV. 'Nervous?' is the message. The responses all suggest they have no expectation of beating Stoke this afternoon.

Soares makes his Stoke City debut and makes an early impact with some pacey runs. On just seven minutes Delap puts Soares in for a great chance, but the shot is scuffed. Stoke are all over Spurs in the opening twenty minutes and Soares goes clear through again. A miss-timed Bale tackle clatters him. There will be fewer more blatant penalties this season and it is given immediately. To make things even better Bale gets a straight red. It is not a malicious tackle, but by the letter of the law he has to be sent off, as he was last man. Higginbotham steps up, but the ball gets blown off the penalty spot. He replaces it and walks back. The ball blows off the penalty spot again as the wind whips through the open corner between the South Stand and the John Smiths Stand. The ball is replaced for a third time, but again it blows off the spot. This is creating unbearable tension in the stadium. Higginbotham places the ball for a fourth time, steps back and cracks it straight past Gomes. You will not see a better penalty under such difficult circumstances and it sends The Brit delirious. Stoke are 1-0 up against ten men. What a chance for three points this afternoon.

Stoke inexplicably then decide to sit back and invite Spurs on. We see this so often, but against ten men you have to question the wisdom. Stoke are punished by a Bent equaliser just five minutes later. Bent is clearly offside, but the deflected pass plays him on. It is against the run of play, but Stoke only have themselves to blame as Spurs are here for the taking now.

Following the re-start Spurs attack again and it is only down to a couple of wide shots and some good keeping from Sorenson that Stoke go in at halftime level.

Words must be said at halftime because Stoke come out fired up. Early on Sidibe is put wide by Soares and he whips in a fabulous cross that is met by Delap who is unmarked and piling in at the far post. Delap and the ball end up in the back up of net with Delap celebrating in the net in front of The Boothen End. It is a fabulous move, a fabulous finish and creates the perfect image of Delap celebrating in the netting in front of our delirious fans. I feel that even with over half an hour to go, Delap's goal will be the decisive one. From that point on, the afternoon falls apart for Spurs.

With half an hour left Hutton gets booked for leaving a foot in on Sorenson who has to be replaced because of a horrible gash to his head. There is a strong argument for another red card. Just minutes later Corluka collapses after being clattered in the face by Gomes. In the immediate aftermath everyone knows it is serious and it takes a full ten minutes of treatment on the pitch in front of The Boothen End. Stoke's fans may be getting a reputation for hostility to their opponents, but in this situation The Boothen End shows its compassion. There is respectful quiet and then applause from all sides of the ground as he is stretchered off. Fuller replaces Kitson, who has had another quiet game.

As a result of injuries there ends up being eleven minutes of stoppage time, but there is not the usual dread that Spurs will get an injury time equaliser. They look a beaten team. Five minutes into injury time another run by Soares sees him floored in the penalty area and Stoke are given a perfect opportunity to kill the game. Fuller steps up and hits the penalty against the inside of the post. The ball goes along the goal line behind Gomes and back out off the inside of the other post into the path of Delap who then blasts it against the cross bar.

A horror tackle by Dawson on Sidibe then sums up the afternoon for Spurs. It is right in front of me and it is an absolute shocker. Sidibe is fortunate not to have a broken leg and Spurs are down to nine men. Fuller takes full advantage of the space a disorganised nine man Spurs creates, beats their defence and cracks a curling thirty yard shot right onto the cross bar. When the game finishes 2-1 there is obvious relief for a valuable three points, but also a feeling that 3-1 or 4-1 would have been a more appropriate score line.

The journey home is filled with distraught and whinging Spurs fans on Talksport and 606. Spurs fans are the world's biggest whingers, but in truth it appears they really do having something to whinge about this year. This is now the worst ever start to a football season in their history and from what we have witnessed today there is a very real chance Spurs will be relegated. It is a view shared by Spurs fans we meet at Warwick services on the M40 and from Spurs friends during the post match text message banter. The general view is that this is the nail in the coffin for Ramos as Spurs manager and that Spurs really are the 'crisis club' of the moment. The win for Stoke takes them above The Premier League's other 'crisis club' this year, Newcastle United.

Man City Away

At the start of the season there are were two games I knew I would not be able to attend unless dates moved for TV. The first was Portsmouth away and the second is this game at Man City. Ironically it is because I am in Portsmouth for the weekend that I cannot attend Man City away. Had the Portsmouth away game fallen on this weekend, then it would have been perfect. As it happens it is very disappointing not to be at Eastlands to watch Stoke play the newly crowned, richest club in the world. The visit to Man City is certainly one of the highlights of the away games this season.

I have been in Portsmouth for The Great South Run. Both my kids took part in the Mini South Run and at this event the FA Cup was on show. I think it is the first time I have actually seen the FA Cup and it is a sign of just how far Portsmouth have come in recent seasons. They are due to play AC Milan in the UEFA cup as a result of winning the FA Cup last season. Is it so hard to imagine Stoke in Europe when you consider teams like Middlesbrough and Portsmouth have done so in recent seasons? Portsmouth is not a happy place this weekend. Ramos did indeed get sacked from Spurs during the week and this morning Harry Redknapp announced he was leaving Portsmouth to become the new manager of Spurs. The locals are fuming in Portsmouth and want Harry's head on a plate.

The Man City away game kicks off as we are driving back home on the M27 so it is going to be a case of staying in touch with the game by mobile phone. Having on Radio 5 Live, instead of the Mamma Mia soundtrack, is not really an option as I am in the minority in the car. It is another Sunday fixture that appears, rather controversially, to have been moved on the advice from Greater Manchester Police. Even though I am two hundred and fifty miles away, my brother and my dad are driving the three hundred and fifty mile round trip from Oxford to go to the game after my brother persuaded my dad to go. At least I will have expert analysis of the game through a Stoke fan's eyes at halftime and fulltime.

Kate has kindly agreed to drive which allows me to refresh the BBC Live Text every thirty seconds for forty five minutes without the risk of crashing the car. My take on the game is that Man City are good for their 1-0 lead at halftime, but Stoke are still in it and have had some good chances. Hope definitely remains in this game. My assessment based on the text version of the game appears pretty accurate when I get the halftime report from the stadium. The only difference is my dad thinks it is without hope and Stoke will get thrashed. Funny, I am sure he said the same at the Villa and Everton home games, so perhaps there is still hope here. The other message is that the Manchester weather is as bad as in Portsmouth and my dad and brother have seats in the front row and are taking the full brunt of the rain. I allow myself a smug smile as I sip my Cappuccino in the warmth of Winchester services and look at the rain lashing down outside.

The first BBC Live Text refresh of the second half shows Robinho has added his second straight from kick off. Stoke will not come back from this and Robinho's brace today means he has reduced his price per goal from ten point eight million pounds to six and a half million pounds per goal. One more and he will look better value than Kitson. A third is indeed added by Robinho for his first Premier League hatrick. The 3-0 victory flatters Man City, as Stoke made some good chances, but today is all about the thirty two and a half million pound man. I speak to my dad after the game. He is contemplating the four hour drive in wet underpants and I am thinking I probably picked a good one to miss.

Sunderland Home

Winter has arrived. The balmy afternoons of late summer when we played Villa and Everton at The Brit are a distant memory. It is an evening kick off and it is sub-zero. It may only be the end of October, but it feels like the middle of January. It is the half-term holidays and Stoke have three games scheduled for half-term week. I have taken the week off work and it is not unusual for us to go away for a couple of days during half term. Kate is still a bit sore about spending August in Manchester and her suggestion that we should go abroad for the whole week needed some rapid intervention on my part.

My first attempt was to try and arrange a few days holiday in The Potteries, with the suggestion of Trentham Monkey Forest, Waterworld and Alton Towers thrown in as a bribe. This initial plan ultimately failed and culminated in a closing argument of, 'Look, if you intend to spend your holidays in Stoke-on-Trent, you'll be doing it alone.' There were probably a few expletives thrown in as well as this is not the first time a Trentham Monkey Forest trip coinciding with a Stoke home game has been suggested. Much as I like The Potteries, trying to persuade someone it is a great family holiday destination is a bit of a challenge. The plan to ensure I get to the Sunderland and Arsenal home games is going to require something a whole lot more devious.

As luck would have it an old friend contacted me a few weeks ago. He also has a young family and lives in Harrogate. We only see them about once a year and we agree it would be great to meet up at half-term. Rather than one of us driving all the way, we decide to meet up halfway and have a few days away together on neutral ground. I offer to make all the arrangements. Without much effort I arrange two nights in The Peak District staying Thursday and Friday night. It is perfect and nobody is any the wiser.

'Buxton?' says Kate looking at the map. 'Buxton isn't half way between Reading and Harrogate.'

'I know, but it's said to be very nice and I thought we could maximise our time up there by having a stop over on the way up on the Wednesday night.'

'Buxton looks pretty close to Stoke.'

'I'll treat you to a really nice hotel in Stoke on the Wednesday.' I lie. I have already booked The Holiday Inn Express at The Britannia Stadium.

Today, as we drive up the M40, Kate is resigned to her fate of having to spend a night in Stoke-on-Trent for the Sunderland home game. The journey up has been a bit fraught because of traffic. I am also nervous because I do not have the parking pass and I am unsure exactly what the parking arrangements are at the hotel on match days. As the M6 traffic crawls past Stafford with the kids in melt down in the back, I have visions of jumping out of the car at 8pm and leaving Kate in the middle of the industrial estates around The Brit trying to park and find the hotel. This potential relationship disaster is adverted when we arrive at the hotel at 7:30pm to find the parking and hotel check-in well organised. I have time to see Kate and the kids safely to the room before a quick dash across the car park sees me in my seat as the teams kick off. The only downside is that in the rush I am not appropriately dressed for a freezing night game at The Brit. There is a strange phenomenon that whatever the temperature is outside, it is always about five degrees colder inside The Britannia Stadium. Thirty seconds into the game I am pretty sure I am going to die of hypothermia.

I am on my own because my dad cannot get back after the game and my brother could not get the time off work, but we are starting to get friendly with fellow season ticket holders. I am asked about my dad. Going to a game on your own can sometimes be a lonely experience, but with season ticket holders you get to know the same faces week in, week out. That said, I do not know them that well and feel obliged to leave an empty seat either side of me and this significantly exacerbates the potential for me to get hypothermia.

The game itself is a 'must win' in terms of relegation and Stoke oblige. It is a game that I really enjoy without it being particularly spectacular. Sunderland, despite huge amounts spent, look like an ordinary side and in truth the game would not have looked out of place in The Championship. The sell-out crowd is the giveaway that this is still The Premier League. If it were a midweek Championship game the ground would be half empty and it is highly likely I would not be freezing my nuts off.

Stoke are well organised and snuff Sunderland out. The single goal comes on seventy three minutes and it is a bullet header from Fuller off the Delap long throw right in front of The Boothen End. It is one to keep the TV pundits focussed on Stoke's direct tactics. Sunderland have chances to equalise, but I genuinely feel that it is a comfortable Stoke win off the back of a very lame Sunderland performance. The win takes Stoke to ten points from ten games and up to fifteenth in The Premier League. Things are looking a lot healthier now.

Usually we can wait anything between thirty and ninety minutes to get out of The South Car Park after a home game. When you have got two hours drive plus a further train journey on top it is incredibly frustrating every week to get stuck in the car park. Not tonight though. Five minutes after leaving my seat I am watching Arsenal v Tottenham in the warmth of the hotel lobby. What a last five minutes it is. Tottenham score two in injury time to take the game to 4-4. Harry Redknapp is working his magic and the bottom of The Premier League is tightening up.

Arsenal Home

It has been an excellent few days since the Sunderland game. The noise from The Brit had kept my girls awake in the hotel and they woke up genuinely excited to have the stadium outside their window in the morning. I had planned to visit Stanley Matthews with them first thing, but the weather made this an unappealing prospect. The hotel was full of Stoke and Sunderland fans and there was much discussion about the game over breakfast. I shall be doing the hotel experience for home evening games again.

We spent the morning after the game in Newcastle and for me it was a trip down memory lane. My mum is from Newcastle and my dad from Silverdale. Until I was seven I would spend every weekend in Newcastle, often helping out my Nan on a Saturday in the laundrette on Merial Street. That was until I was deemed old enough to go to the match with my dad. I am sure he took pride in taking his son to The Victoria Ground, but for him he had to change his pre-match routine of meeting his mates in The Museum on George Street before heading off down to Stoke. He also gave up The Boothen End for a while and we sat in The Butler Street Stand until I was tall enough to see. Even after we moved south in 1979 we would still visit Newcastle at least once a month and more often during the football season. This continued to happen until about ten years ago when the last of my grand parents passed on. Despite regular trips for football and the occasional trip for work, it is at least ten years since I visited Newcastle properly and more like fifteen since I actually spent a night in North Staffs. As such I make no apology for some serious reminiscing as I eat my oatcakes in Brampton Park and watch my kids play in the same place that I did thirty years ago. It has not actually changed much.

Forty eight hours later and I have been dropped on the A53 and am walking up Waterloo Road into Hanley. The couple of days in Buxton and The Peak District have been great, but Kate is keen to get back to Oxford as the girls are getting their bridesmaid dresses fitted for Kate's sister's wedding. Kate had been reluctant to give me a lift back to Stoke from Buxton and it was looking like being a couple of hours by service bus via Leek at one point. Eventually she agreed to divert her journey home and I have been dropped outside Hanley at 10am with five hours to kill before kick off. I am pretty sure I have not been to Hanley for nearly twenty years, so it is going to be another trip down memory lane in preparation for what is one of our biggest home games of the season.

Armed with a Sentinal and selection of national papers I settle down for a fry-up and oatcakes in the café on Cheapside as I contemplate today's game. Arsenal is huge for Stoke fans. In recent years Manchester United has become the team we all love to hate, but in the early seventies it was Arsenal that stood in the way when Stoke's moment nearly arrived. Beaten in two consecutive FA Cup semi-final replays, it is Arsenal that haunts those that are old enough to remember the early seventies. I settle my own pre-match nerves with a visit to Hanley museum followed by a couple of pints in The Walkabout whilst watching the first half of Everton v Fulham. Then it is over to The Brit nice and early. My dad and brother are running late because of traffic and will only arrive just before kick off. I sense tension in the car. I head inside on my own and watch the rest of the Everton v Fulham game in the concourse.

With points now on the board and expectation of beating Arsenal pretty low, pre-match I feel relaxed. This is a day to enjoy. The stress of 'must win' games can wait for another day. The game is of course another sell-out and the pre-match atmosphere is once again fired up. Arsenal field a line up of world-beaters, but there is a question mark over their bottle in recent seasons. Today should prove the ultimate test and it seems obvious to me after just a few minutes when Arsenal's defence fail to deal with the first Delap long throw that it will be a test that Arsenal will fail. It takes just eleven minutes for Stoke to take a deserved lead with Fuller glancing a header in off the second Delap long throw of the afternoon. Arsenal are just not in the game and Stoke have a couple of good chances to extend their lead before halftime. Adebayor leaves a foot in on Shawcross and is lucky to receive just a yellow card. It sums up the frustration from Arsenal.

The second half sees Arsenal searching for an equaliser. Sorenson makes some decent saves and again Abdoulaye Faye stands out. He is making an early case for our player of the season. Arsenal appear ineffective and with half an hour left Wenger brings on van Persie and recent England hatrick hero Walcott. This changes the game and the pace injected by both players now looks threatening, although in truth Arsenal still appear lightweight as Stoke take the robust approach to holding their lead. This culminates in a nasty late challenge on Adebayor by Shawcross. It is one that Stoke's favourite referee, Rob Styles, misses and minutes later Adebayor hobbles off. On his way off the pitch Shawcross lifts his shorts to show Adebayor the stud marks left on him earlier in the game. Point made, but Shawcross is probably fortunate not to be booked.

On seventy three minutes there is another long throw that Arsenal completely fail to deal with and Olofinjana first chests the ball to the floor and then bundles it into the back of the net with his face as he falls to the ground. It is not going to be short-listed for Goal Of The Season, but it is one of the most important goals of the season for Stoke and the stadium erupts. Back in the summer I did not dare dream that we would be beating teams like Arsenal, but in truth the ease in which Stoke are now winning the game actually means the celebrations feel a little muted given the magnitude of what is going on.

With fifteen minutes left the ball goes to Sorenson, who holds onto it. Stoke are in no rush now and this clearly frustrates van Persie, who in a red mist charges Sorenson with his shoulder. It is not particularly dangerous, but there will not be a clearer or more stupid sending off all season. It is one that Styles obliges with a red card much to the delight and taunting of the Stoke fans. The away end empties. The Gooners have seen enough and they head for their coaches soundly beaten with ten minutes of the game remaining. I am sure the majority of the Arsenal fans do not see the late cynical trip by Delap on Walcott. It is not dirty, but an awkward fall sees the England man stretchered off with what looks like a serious shoulder injury. Arsenal score a undeserved goal from a deflected free kick as a result of the foul by Delap, but down to nine men and deep into injury time it really is nothing more than a consolation. The Arsenal fans know this and a lack passion in the goal celebration even makes me think the goal has been disallowed. It is not, but the game is lost and it is a famous victory for Stoke. More crucially it is three more unexpected points in the relegation battle.

My brother has already left to get the early train back to London so I head to the car park with my dad for the drive back to Oxford. The Arsenal fans we encounter look shell-shocked and on the drive back 606 is full of suggestion that Arsenal's lack of guile has seen them drop out of the championship race. Wenger does not accept this of course, but he plays credit to Stoke in the post match interviews. For the second time in three weeks we are driving back down the M40 with North London supporters who are feeling the ill effects of a visit to The Britannia Stadium and it feels brilliant. I hook up with Kate back in Oxford and for once she shares the delight. She has been with Gooner Jon, my future brother in law, doing wedding preparation and they have been following the events unfolding at The Brit. Jon is nowhere to be seen by the time I arrive. Funny that, but I will make sure he gets some stick next time I see him.

The win against Arsenal has defined our season. No matter what happens now, Stoke have scalped one of the big four. Stoke's direct, aggressive style of play and the passion of the home fans has destroyed Arsenal's chances of winning the league. When the end of season review is written, any beautiful football that Stoke do play will be forgotten and the focus will be on the direct and aggressive tactics fired up by passionate home support. Frankly if we avoid relegation we will take it that way and hold the rare moments of magic, like Fuller's goal against Villa, sacred. For Arsenal though, you need to come to places like Stoke-on-Trent and meet fire with fire. Arsenal play the beautiful game beautifully, but it counts for little if you cannot play the beautiful game ugly when it matters. Arsenal have shown they do not have the bottle to play against the teams scrapping against relegation.

Wigan Away

It has all gone off in the week. The credit Wenger paid Stoke directly after the game quickly evaporated once Arsenal returned to London to lick their wounds. In Wenger's midweek press conference the claims that Stoke are a dirty side come flooding out and the press are quick to pick up on it. Frankly, who cares? It is the points that matter for Stoke, not how they are won. The fact that most of Wenger's claims are without merit makes it look like a serious case of sour grapes.

Kate has finally cracked in terms of me spending every weekend at football leaving her with the kids all day at weekends. Having had the summer and autumn holidays dominated by the football fixtures, the subject of Christmas was discussed this week. To be fair to Kate the Boxing Day football always dominates plans in our household, but this year December and January are packed with games. I won the battle over Christmas fixtures because many of our away games are in London and Kate's sister's wedding falls on FA Cup third round day for which there has been a three line whip for the last nine months. Even so, I think there will have to be some concessions on away games in November and December.

A few weeks ago Kate was planning bonfire night. We were all keen to go to fireworks as a family on one of the Saturdays that spanned November 5th. Realistically this meant missing either Arsenal at home or Wigan away. Not a difficult decision, but once the Wigan kick off was brought forward to midday on police advice, I bought a ticket anyway on the assumption that I would be able to get back to Reading from Wigan with plenty of time to spare for fireworks. Network Rail, who once again closed the lines going north on the Saturday, scuppered that plan. I raised the possibility of taking the family car and it was this that was the catalyst for Kate's vocal expression of her unhappiness at being a football widow every Saturday. This made Wigan away concession number one. In hasty last minute arrangements my dad takes my ticket and drives with my brother to Wigan for the game. I am at Legoland in the rain for the fireworks.

I get ninety minutes of respite from the Legoland experience to follow the game on BBC Live Text. The game kicks off at 12:45pm, the same time as Arsenal v Liverpool. BBC Live Text is ninety nine percent dominated by Arsenal versus Liverpool and initially I am livid at the bias of the BBC. However, it soon becomes obvious that there is very little to report from the JJB Stadium. This is confirmed at halftime when my dad suggests it is one of the worst games he has ever seen. It turns out to be a very poor 0-0 draw, with Stoke deploying negative spoiling tactics and Wigan unable to break down Stoke's defence. Sorenson is the hero in a game that Wigan could, and maybe should, have won. It is shown last on Match Of The Day. It does however provide Stoke with a valuable away point, their second of the season. Fourteen points from twelve games and the early kick off sees Stoke temporarily into the top half of the table. Once the weekend's fixtures are completed just five points separate the bottom twelve teams in what is now officially the closest Premier League competition since it began.

Rotherham Home

The last sixteen of The League Cup sees Stoke drawn at home to Rotherham who are struggling in the football's fourth tier. It is a good crowd at The Britannia bolstered by a healthy following from Rotherham. I am not amongst the crowd. Stoke in the last sixteen of a cup competition is rare, but it is not going to tempt me to the three hundred mile round trip that requires an afternoon off work. Stoke field a number of players that have been sidelined this season. Most notably, Kitson starts after losing his starting place to the Fuller / Sidibe combination in the league. There are also starts for Pugh and Whelan and it is Pugh and Whelan who score the goals in a comfortable 2-0 win for Stoke. Stoke are in the quarterfinals of a cup competition for the first time in thirty years. Dare we start dreaming of silverware and Europe? The cup draw will be made on Saturday, the day we travel up to Old Trafford.

Man United Away

This is the big one. No matter how much we try and play down Manchester United, this game will have been the first one the majority of Stoke fans would have looked for when The Premier League fixtures were announced in June. I have not been to Old Trafford since 1985 when Stoke were thrashed 5-0 in their relegation season. Manchester United, Old Trafford and football in general have changed beyond recognition in the twenty three years since our last league game there. I know tourists and corporates now pack the seats where once the Stretford End terrace and North Stand paddock intimidated the away fans. I also know that I need to enjoy the experience, have little expectation about the result and not get carried away with pre-conceived ideas of the modern day Old Trafford. After all with match tickets costing an astronomical fifty quid and train tickets to and from the south at a premium because of The Cockney Reds, today is a very, very expensive day out. Stoke have sold their maximum ticket allocation, but tickets did not sell out as quickly as I had expected. I think a lot of Stoke fans are starting to feel The Premier League pinch.

The day starts well enough. I get into London from Reading, but with time a bit tight I have to hop in a cab from Paddington to Euston to get the 10am departure for Manchester. As always in London the cabbie supports West Ham and he is more than happy to offer his opinion on Stoke's season so far, particularly in relation to the Arsenal and Tottenham victories. He has a pretty raw view on Arsene Wenger. He also has a pretty raw view on Man United, Ferguson and Ronaldo. In fact he has a pretty raw view on pretty much everything. I meet my brother as his cab pulls into the Euston cab rank behind mine. He too was running late from Hammersmith. He is carrying a Kevin Keegan fancy dress costume complete with skin-tight Admiral England shirt from the 1982 world cup. It is for a fancy dress party back in London after the game. I desperately try and persuade him to wear it to the match, but he is having none of it and it is checked into left luggage for later. There is just time to buy breakfast before getting on the train.

Today it is first class. We are not being flash, but once again, inexplicably the advance first class fares were cheaper than standard class fares. It makes for a pleasant journey, which is fortunate, because with weekend engineering works it will take nearly four hours as we get diverted via Birmingham. The train is full of Man United fans, many of whom appear to be South East Asian tourists. With the exception of the odd Icelandic tourist, football tourism has not really taken off at The Britannia Stadium, so it is a strange phenomenon to witness and goes to show what a truly global brand Manchester United is. I had expected a few Stoke fans on board travelling up from London, but there are none visible. When we pass through Stoke station it is surprising that the platform is pretty much deserted. I had expected hundreds of Stoke fans to board, but there aren't any. They must have got earlier trains.

Whilst I respect Man United as a football club, as any football fan surely has to, I do reserve a special deep-rooted hatred for their fans. Man United are not England. On the very rare occasions I can be bothered to watch The Champions League, I support the foreign teams when they play Man United. I wanted Bayern Munich to win in 1999 and I nearly cried as much as John Terry back in May. This is nothing to do with Man United as a football club, it is simply down to how I feel about their fans. Given that they have got a few million worldwide, that is a fairly generic and ridiculous statement to make, so I should probably be more specific. I hate the fans who live in Berkshire, Oxfordshire, Kent, Surrey and Essex who only watch Man United on the TV and were the ones wearing their replica shirts in the playgrounds of South East England when I grew up as a kid. In truth most of them probably now support Chelsea. However it seems there are still a lot of southern Man United glory hunters on this train.

The League Cup quarterfinal draw is being made during the journey and having been identified as Stoke fans in our carriage we become engaged with a number of the Man United fans on the subject of The League Cup. There is one girl in particular who it turns out is actually from Manchester. Despite now living in London, she goes home and away with Man United. On hearing this I have to adjust my pre-conceptions about some of the Man United fans travelling up from London for the game. I have to accept she is a proper football fan and more to the point she is very friendly which would make it inappropriate to go off on one about Man United not respecting the domestic cup competitions. Stoke draw Derby at home in The League Cup. What an opportunity for Stoke to progress.

We arrive at Manchester Piccadilly and jump in a cab to a pub in Deansgate. We are meeting Lee, Matt and one of Matt's mates. They all support Man United and are my brother's mates who he met when he was in Australia. Lee is a genuine Manc and season ticket holder at Old Trafford. Matt and his mate are from Milton Keynes. It turns out that although the MK boys claim to be life long Man United fans, today is their first ever visit to Old Trafford. It seems tourist football is not reserved just for South East Asia, but extends to Milton Keynes as well. Lee is expertly playing the role of arrogant Man United fan and reminiscing about the big European nights at Old Trafford. He apologies that the Man United fans will not be up for it today as it is only Stoke. He claims it is difficult to get excited about The Championship teams when you are used to playing Real Madrid and Barcelona. Deep down we all know Man United cannot afford any slip-ups today if they want to apply pressure to Liverpool and Chelsea at the top of the table. We leave it late before getting a cab to Old Trafford. No visits to The Munich Memorial today as we are still in the pub at 2:40pm. We take our seats in Old Trafford right on 3pm and it is fair to say Old Trafford is an awe-inspiring sight although the only real noise is that generated by Stoke's support. One thing that really strikes me is the camera flashes. It feels more like an American sports event than an English football match.

Almost immediately Man United get a free kick in a dangerous position. Ronaldo steps up and hammers it straight at Sorenson. As I look away to see where Sorenson can release the ball to, I am momentarily unaware that the ball has gone through Sorenson and into the back of the net. The wall of noise from Old Trafford hits us and I look at the referee in futile hope that we are going to see a repeat of Gerrard at Anfield. Not a chance and having travelled six hours to get here, it seems Stoke have already blown it, just three minutes after my arrival at the stadium. The Stoke fans get up behind the team and console themselves with barracking Ronaldo. When Ronaldo reacts to the Stoke fans with some petulant arm waving it just increases the volume of abuse. The purists might suggest it is inappropriate to single players out for abuse, but there is nothing racist or family related being hurled at Ronaldo so I think it is fair game, particularly given Ronaldo's reputation for petulance. Frankly, provoking the worst side of probably the best player in The Premier League is very satisfying. Stoke settle, defend well and even have a chance to pull level. I head downstairs on forty three minutes to top up the beers at halftime.

'1-0 isn't too bad', I say as my brother joins me in the concourse.

'You didn't see Carrick's goal then?' I check for signs of a wind up, but there are none. 2-0 down at Old Trafford and it is damage limitation time.

We get back to our seats just in time to see Berbatov score Man United's third and it is tempting to leave there and then. Stoke hold out for a further thirty five minutes without making any real chances and the Stoke fans amuse themselves by trying to wind up Ronaldo again. Ferguson throws on the kids for the final few minutes and Danny Wellbeck rounds off a humiliating afternoon by scoring a rocket. His first goal for Man United and there will be few better. I have had enough and we head to the exit with five minutes remaining in a plan to beat the other seventy five thousand back to The South East.

We get a train back to Manchester Piccadilly from right behind the away section and we are back in Manchester by 5:10pm. There is some good banter on the train, but the confirmation that the final score ended up 5-0 with Ronaldo getting the fifth means most of the banter is one way. Stoke have been outclassed and we have experienced our first Premier League humiliation. It is gutting, but relegation will not be avoided on days like today. Apart from the goal difference taking a hammering, in the grand scheme of things the result does not matter that much. I am now keen to mull over the humiliation on a comfortable train journey back to London.

Manchester Piccadilly station has been transformed into a fortress. With trouble reported at Bolton, Liverpool, Wigan and Man City this season, it seems that Greater Manchester Police are up for a bit of heavy handed policing this evening. It is also pretty apparent that the station is dry with all bars closed. I seek out the friendliest looking WPC I can find and ask her where a neutral can get a drink for an hour or two before catching the train to London. I get an initial look like I am about to be battened, but she asks her colleague and we are told of a small pub behind the station that is open for locals. We are also told to stay off the station until our train is due. We find the pub and it is obviously open, but the doors are locked. In our failed attempts to find a way in we manage to clearly identify ourselves as being not local. Eventually the landlord opens the door. 'Sorry lads, locals only.'

'Please, we only want a quick pint, no trouble.'

'Sorry lads.'

With little else to do we return to the station. My brother heads to Sainsbury's to get takeouts for the journey home and I head to KFC. We arrange to meet on the train in our reserved seats. KFC in hand I head to the platform from where the London train is departing and it is utter chaos. It appears the police are not letting some people on the train and yet forcing others on board even if they do not actually want to get on. I try and circumvent the main aggravation whilst showing my ticket in the air, but I get 'Oi, what's your game?'

'Just getting my train. I've got a reservation.'

'Who do you support?' This is tricky as I am unsure what is going on and I suspect the police are preventing Stoke fans travelling on this train.

'I'm not a football fan. I've got a reservation for this train to London. I have to get it.' The delay in my answer has aroused suspicion and now I am nervous that this particular copper is looking for a quick snatch to get himself back in the van and away from the trouble that is brewing on the platform.

'The train's de-classified smart arse. Do you want to get nicked?'

'Look, I'm a neutral. I have a ticket and a reservation that has to be used on this train.'

'Take it up with Virgin Trains. One last time, are you Stoke or United?' All Virgin Trains staff are conspicuous by their absence. I am pretty sure I am going to get nicked here.

'Stoke.' I say fearing the worst.

'Not too difficult was it?' he says smugly, 'Back of the train.'

Not too difficult? It would have been far easier to have a sign saying away fans at the back, home fans at the front. It worked well enough at Bolton away, so why the aggravation here? Anyway I quit while I am ahead and get on the train.

I find our carriage, but there's no way I can get to our

reserved seats and there is no sign of my brother. I call him and the police are holding him on the platform. 'Tell them you support Stoke and have to get this train'. I can hear frantic discussion going on in the background. The train is about to depart and I consider getting off. I hear the copper say 'What, your brother's on the train?' Too late, the train departs. A few minutes later my brother appears through the crowd of Stoke fans rammed in the first class carriages. He is not happy. GMP have treated him pretty badly and they confiscated all the booze he bought. Now we are packed in a train for four hours without even so much as a soft drink available. It is not a pleasant prospect.

There is some momentary calm once the train arrives in Stoke. The majority of fans in our carriage get off and we find our reserved seats. There is a young women travelling alone sitting at our table and I get a glance from her like we have sat there to give her hassle. 'Our reserved seats, sorry.' I say trying to give my friendliest non-football hooligan smile.

'No problem,' she says, 'I wasn't expecting this when my company paid for my first class return ticket. I've been working at a conference all week in Manchester and was looking forward to chilling out with a magazine and a glass of wine. Do you support Stoke as well?'

'Yeah, but don't hold that against us.'

'I'm Anna. The lads sat here before were dead friendly and really funny.'

'Well I can't promise that, but you'll get no hassle from me. Can't say the same for my brother though.'

It turns out Anna is up for some conversation to kill the boredom of the journey. The calm is disturbed when the train departs Stoke as The Cockney Reds pile into first class. There are now no police and no Virgin train staff to prevent a free for all. A nutter in his late forties takes the fourth seat at our table. We are immediately clocked as Stoke and within ten minutes we are given his very frank views on 'Stoke scum', 'thieving Scousers', 'the Hillsborough disaster' and his string of convictions for football related violence all while he is trying to get a good look down Anna's top. I can't suss out whether this guy is genuine, but he does look like he is carrying a few scars from the early eighties. The culture of football hooliganism can sometimes carry an intriguing fascination, but this guy is simply making me feel sick. He is looking for a reaction from us and I am not going to give him the satisfaction. His claims that his crew are raiding the closed buffet car seem unfounded. I am pretty sure he is travelling alone and when he finally departs at Watford I can see no sign of any crew. There is a serious release of tension at our table and my brother turns his attention to trying to persuade Anna to come to the fancy dress party as Mrs. Keegan.

Back at Euston I am dehydrated and even a quick hug and peck on the cheek from Anna doesn't really lift my post match blues. Anna heads home and I cannot even summon the energy for one for the road in Euston. My brother heads reluctantly to Camden for the party he now cannot really be bothered with and I head back to Paddington to catch the train to Reading. Ultimately it has been a pretty disastrous day, ruined by a sterile Old Trafford atmosphere, a humiliation for Stoke, a shocking journey home and serious money laid out. Would relegation and a return to The Championship really be so bad?

West Brom Home

We always beat West Brom. Stoke's record against West Brom really is uncanny, so what better way to recover from the Old Trafford humiliation than with a home game against our local rivals. After a bright start West Brom are now bottom of the league. The media appear to be talking up the beautiful football of West Brom whilst continuing to ridicule the style of Stoke. The reality is that West Brom are not very good and Mowbray appears tactically naive about what it is going to take to keep them in The Premier League. Pulis on the other hand does seem to be working wonders with limited resources, especially at home and is adopting a more pragmatic 'win at all cost' approach even if the end result is not always particularly pretty. As a result the bookmakers now have West Brom as firm favourites for the drop, but Stoke are still not far behind in the prices. Today is not the day for losing the twenty six year unbeaten home record to The Baggies. However there could be a problem getting three points because Stoke have not really been tested by a team coming to The Britannia and defending for a draw. There remains a serious question as to whether Stoke have the creativity to break teams down, especially today without Fuller and Lawrence.

At halftime the answer to that question is a resounding no. Fuller is conveniently serving his one-match ban whilst on international duty. This is the opportunity Kitson has been waiting for. He is stretchered off with a knee injury early in the game as his season goes from promising to worrying to disastrous. Miller looks dangerous, but West Brom look like they could play for a week and not score. Even Delap's throws are not looking particularly effective and rumours that he is carrying a shoulder injury appear to be true. This game has an awful 0-0 encounter written all over it.

The second half sees more of the same with Stoke limited to half chances and a reasonable shout for a penalty. A defensive error creates West Brom's best chance of the game, but it is spurned. With ten minutes left I start to get that sinking feeling that today our record against West Brom will end. 'I'll take a draw now' I say to my brother and he agrees. Five minutes left and the first quality move of the game sees Higginbotham and Tongue split open the West Brom defence. The cross finds an unmarked Sidibe, who loops his inch perfect header over the defence and into the opposite bottom corner of the goal. This sparks relief and delirious celebrations at The Britannia. There are even a couple of Boothen Enders on the pitch. It is late in the game, but to be honest I think Stoke could have played until midnight and not conceded.

Four home wins in a row and seventeen points from fourteen games sees Stoke thirteenth in the table. Seventeen points is a major landmark. In 1984/5 Stoke got seventeen points all season and that was with four extra games. Sunderland and Derby have since done worse, but in 1985 that was the all time low. Whatever happens now it will not be worse than 1984/5 as many had predicted back in May. On the drive back to Oxford we are entertained by Mowbray's deluded post match comments regarding West Brom's flowing style being subdued by Stoke's aggressive and negative tactics. From what I saw West Brom were the negative tacticians today. When all is said and done we all know tactics are irrelevant in this fixture because whatever happens we always beat West Brom.

Hull Home

As fellow Premier League virgins, Hull have rather annoyingly taken the limelight so far this season. I had hoped that today would be the day that order would be restored and Stoke would go above Hull in The Premier League. With Hull having beaten Newcastle, Arsenal and Tottenham away amongst their six league wins so far, it looked like their bubble had burst at the end of October just as Stoke were hitting some real form. With Stoke now having the luxury of a sneaky glance up into the top half of the league table, we can see that two recent draws for Hull still puts them five points ahead of Stoke. More interesting though, is that a Stoke win today could see them climb to seventh in the table.

Unlike the straightforward travel for West Brom last week, today is generating rather more stress. I had arranged to meet my brother at Reading station at about 11am to share a relaxed train journey over to Oxford. Instead it is now 12:15pm and I am still waiting for him. Delays on the Hammersmith & City Line have pushed back his arrival. He was close to bailing out of the match completely and now it will be a close thing to make the kick off. We eventually meet my dad in Oxford at 12:55pm and after a hectic drive north, we arrive at The Brit at 2:45pm. I drop them by the Audi garage and park up in The South Car Park. I know that any chance of a quick, post match getaway has been scuppered by our late arrival.

The game itself starts off slowly, but Stoke have most of the possession and carve open a few half chances in the first half hour. It is looking like being another scrappy game that will certainly not be a main feature on Match Of The Day. The only notable highlight of the first half is the gamesmanship organised by Brown and executed by Windass. Windass deliberately warms up in front of Delap as he prepares for his long throw. The second time he is booked without even being on the pitch, much to the delight of the Stoke fans. It is against the run of play when Hull score in first half injury time. Hull have been played off the park so many times this season and still got a result. The Premier League gods are shining down on them and I am absolutely fuming at halftime.

The second half sees Stoke fired up by the injustice of being behind to Hull and although they do not create many chances, there is enough to suggest it will only be a matter of time before they get the equaliser. My attention to the game keeps getting distracted by Brown. He seems more intent on facing off to The Boothen End than he does on watching the game. The more The Boothen End try and wind him up, the more he does it, so The Boothen End try and wind him up even more. He keeps staring and puffing his chest out at the Stoke fans. It is one of the strangest things I have ever seen at a football match. Brown is a controversial figure and his introduction to The Premier League as a darling of the media is now starting to wane after some comical post match interviews and delusions of grandeur. Many fans in The Championship thought he was an idiot, but up to now I have thought him worthy of respect for getting Hull into The Premier League. Today though, for the first time, I can see properly why so many fans deride him.

Stoke's dominance of the game, particularly in the second half is not getting them back on level terms and I am really starting to fear the worst. A Sidibe long ball puts Fuller clear through. The Hull keeper misses his challenge and connects with Fuller's legs for a blatant penalty. There is a split second of anxiety. Fuller has gone down like a sack of spuds when he might have been able to stay on his feet, but the referee awards the penalty. Despite the Hull players' attempts to delay the kick and distract Fuller, he steps up and coolly despatches the spot kick. 1-1 and with fifteen minutes left I am pretty sure Stoke will find the winner. It does not happen and in truth there is a suggestion that Stoke might be happy with a draw today. Hull are certainly happy with a draw and there is plenty of gamesmanship in the last few minutes as Hull waste time. The Hull players even start using Delap's towel to dry the ball.

At the start of the season a draw at home to Hull would have been disastrous, but given Stoke's current run of form it is a satisfactory result after a very mediocre game. In the car park we are in for a long wait, but for once there is some lively post-match entertainment on the radio. Firstly Brown's post match interview on Radio 5 is a complete joke. He accuses Stoke of gamesmanship and Fuller of diving. He has a pop at the referee and suggests Hull should have won by a country mile. Pulis gives his normal levelheaded post match interview. Respect to Pulis, zero respect to Brown. This all sparks a hugely entertaining Stoke versus Hull debate on 606. Call after call sees Stoke against Hull and is far more entertaining than the usual whinging of Spurs and Everton or the arrogance of Man United and Chelsea. There is a general acceptance that Stoke and Hull have brought a breath of fresh air to a stagnant Premier League. After today though I really hope it is temporary for Brown and Hull City. After all, any fans that sing, 'You're getting mauled by the tigers,' whilst using their hands as claws, have no place in the top flight of English football.

Derby Home

Three days later and we are heading back to The Brit for The League Cup quarterfinal. Under the normal circumstances of a mediocre Championship season, this game would be massive, but as we all know this season is not normal. Even so, I still think it is one of the biggest games in Stoke's recent history. For the first time in thirty years, or to put it into personal context, my lifetime as a Stoke fan, Stoke are in the last eight of a major cup competition. There is serious talk of Stoke in Europe next season. So much so, that I have already started dropping hints to Kate about a European adventure for Stoke. Any such away trips will require serious groundwork at home, so I may as well start early.

Stoke are playing Derby, whose disastrous Premier League form last season has continued into The Championship. Derby are fighting double drop relegation and the game for them is the only ray of light in a bleak season so far. It is of course also a local derby and four thousand Derby fans will make the short trip along the A50. The evening kick off means an afternoon off work and I have told my brother I will pick him up from Reading station at 4pm. We will have plenty of time to drive over to Oxford and pick up my dad. Me driving is the only option given that we will not get back until the early hours, when the last train from Oxford to Reading will be long gone. I am therefore pretty livid when my brother does not get to Reading until well after 5pm. There is pretty much no chance of making the kick off now.

My dad is not well and given the weather he pulls out of the match, but we still need to stop at Oxford on our way to get the car park pass. We do not get on the M40 until gone 6pm so any traffic delays will mean we could miss most of the first half. My brother tucks into his crisps and sausage roll, most of which is distributed around the car. He is testing my patience today. We actually get to Junction 15 of the M6 in record time and are on the A50 approach by 7:30pm, but just as hopes are raised that we might make the kick off, they are quickly dashed because of gridlock around The Britannia stadium. The influx of Derby fans appears to have caused traffic chaos on the A50. It is another forty five minutes before we get to our seats.

Surprisingly The Brit is far from sold out, but even with over twenty thousand inside, there is a flat atmosphere for the first time this season and the Stoke fans are being out sung by the large Derby following. None of the usual faces are in our row. There is confirmation from a new face sitting next to me that I have missed nothing significant so far. The side is not full strength with Sorenson and Abdoulaye Faye rested, but it looks strong enough to beat Derby with Sidibe and Fuller up front. Whelan and Cresswell also make rare starts and it is Cresswell who fires Stoke ahead on thirty five minutes in what is the first significant action that I witness. The goal is controversially ruled out. It is unclear why and it is only then that I realise it is Rob Styles refereeing. He may have shown some rare kindness to Stoke in the Arsenal game, but tonight normal service has resumed. It remains 0-0 at halftime as the snow starts to fall heavily on already frozen ground. Getting home could be difficult.

The second half is dire. The crowd is flat, it is freezing and there is little to suggest that this is a game that will see the winner just one tie from Wembley. Both teams have half chances, but it really is another poor home performance that sees Stoke unable to break down a resilient opposition. A worrying pattern is starting to emerge and the first signs of unease about Pulis' tactics are starting to raise their head. Another awful freezing thirty minutes seems inevitable as injury time passes by. Enter the saviour Rob Styles. He obviously does not fancy another thirty minutes either and in the very last minute of injury time he awards a penalty. At the time I am as bewildered as anyone as to why it has been awarded, but it has been. As a roar from the visitors confirms our cup exit, I am already making my way back through the car park. My phone buzzes with gloating texts from Derby fans.

Having left before the final whistle and run back to the car, we actually get away quite quickly for once. Listening to Radio Stoke there is confirmation that it probably was a Griffin handball and although our exit is controversial, Stoke got what they deserved after another uncreative home performance. I am starting to worry that Stoke's negative tactical approach and the lack of creativity we have witnessed away from home is starting to now affect the home performances. I think Stoke could be in for a difficult few months.

We get back to Oxford just after midnight and I drop my brother on the outskirts of town to catch the coach to London. Although the service is twenty four hour it is not regular in the earlier hours and my brother has been hinting all the way down the M40 about me driving him back to London. This would add an extra hour to my journey, but given the alternative is for him to wait up to an hour in the freezing cold for a coach that might not arrive, I am tempted to help him out. He confirms his coach is due any minute so I leave him at the bus stop. Two miles down the M40 I pass his coach heading into London. He has missed it and will have to wait an hour. I nearly turn back, but then catch sight of pastry in the foot well and crisps all over the dashboard. As I drive home across The Chilterns I do not feel quite guilty about leaving him. It is a very disappointing night, but The League Cup is a distraction to the primary business of avoiding relegation. If Stoke do not have the desire to easily beat a poor Derby side at home, they do not deserve to progress.

Newcastle Away

'I think it would be nice to go away for a family weekend break before Christmas,' Kate says.

'OK, sounds nice.' I say knowing that every weekend between now and Christmas involves a Stoke game. 'How about Newcastle?' I suggest.

'Don't even think about it,' is the answer.

So this is how I came to be in Glasgow on the weekend that Stoke are away in Newcastle. I can accept it in part because last season my brother and I had the full on away day experience at St. James' Park with beers, hotel, For Your Eyes Only etc. when Stoke played Newcastle in the FA Cup third round replay. I say in part because today my brother is with Geordie Jamie on the train from Kings Cross to Newcastle to have a full on away day experience at St. James' Park with beers, hotel, For Your Eyes Only etc. and I am pretty gutted not to be with them. Instead I am in Glasgow transport museum looking at old steam trains. It is not a bad museum, but St. James' Park it is not.

By 3pm we are back in our hotel room and a quick chat with my brother confirms that vast amounts of lager have indeed been consumed on the train. However this provides virtually no insight into the game's pre-match build up and with no Sky Sports in the hotel room I have to watch Score instead and try to follow the game via Garth Crooks' posh voiced punditry. There should be hope today as Newcastle are a total shambles this season. When we visited St. James' Park last season Stoke were spanked 4-1 by a resurgent Newcastle, under the watchful eye of the newly re-instated Kevin Keegan.

How quickly things change. Newcastle cannot find a manager, cannot find a buyer and are staring into The Championship abyss. We keep hearing 'Newcastle are too good to go down' which makes them excellent relegation candidates in my view. Their fans also still have delusions of qualifying for Europe and cannot accept they are in a relegation dogfight. I really think they may not have the stomach for it if it really goes to the wire. As my Geordie mate at work said to me this week, 'The number one rule of supporting Newcastle is to ignore reality'. It is the perfect pre-cursor to a genuine relegation six pointer.

Unfortunately though it is Stoke's defence that is a shambles today and Owen appears to have won the game in under half an hour, with two clinical finishes after Stoke's defence was split open. All of a sudden I am not so worried about missing the game because with Stoke lacking any creativity, through negative team selection, it sounds like it is one to miss. My brother confirms it is an awful first half performance from Stoke and he is considering leaving at halftime. With Kate starting to get agitated by the background noise of 'football babble' I turn off the TV and my phone. We head out into Glasgow for tea.

We have settled down for a family meal in Bella Italia and at 5:15pm I get the chance to check the final score on the BBC website. I have got six missed calls from my dad and brother and when I see the Premier League scores I immediately understand why. I skim through the match report and call my brother back.

'Mate, unbelievable,' he says manically, 'you missed a classic. Game of two halves. The Stoke boys have never celebrated like that. It was absolutely mental.'

'What's the matter?' asks Kate.

'Stoke have got a draw at Newcastle', I tell her.

'I thought it was something important. We're eating, talk to your brother later.'

'Nice one,' I say down the phone, 'I'll speak to you later,

have a few for me tonight.'

I finally get to piece together the game on Match Of The Day later that night. The phrase 'game of two halves' was invented for this match. Stoke were dead and buried at halftime after an inept first half performance. Enter Fuller, Whelan and Tonge plus a bit of positive approach play and Stoke play Newcastle off the park in the second half. Stoke's fourth away point of the season is well deserved after the best spell of football away from home this season. Sidibe scores a tap in following a superb Fuller dribble and pass to give Stoke hope. Stoke create numerous chances to draw level and Newcastle look like they have cracked under the pressure.

When the equaliser comes it is as controversial as it is dramatic. Deep into injury time Fuller wins a free kick that looks soft. It sees Newcastle's temporary manager Joe Kinnear sent to the stands for remonstrating with the fourth official. Whelan's perfect delivery finds Abdoulaye Faye, who fires home his first Stoke goal. What a time and what a place to do it and you can see the delight in Faye's face as he celebrates in front of the shell-shocked Newcastle fans. It must mean so much to Faye to hurt the club that released him in the summer. Cue a shot of the Stoke fans celebrating and it is total bedlam. How I wish I had been there.

Fulham Home

More travel problems today, although with my brother at another wedding he is not the one to blame. I was relaxing with a cup of tea and a bacon sandwich on my usual match day train from Reading to Oxford. It did not move from the station and was then inexplicably terminated at Reading. After some rapid platform hopping and phone calls, I finally hook up with my dad about 12:30pm. It is another rush up the M6 to make the kick off. Frankly we need not have bothered.

Stoke's worrying lack of creativity is evident again as they fail to break down Fulham. Apart from Stoke, Fulham have the worst away record in the league having scored just twice away from home all season. Given Stoke's lack of creativity and Fulham's inability to score away from home is it really a surprise that this game ends up being a truly awful 0-0 draw? You could have put your mortgage on it.

With Lawrence still out because of the dog related injury and Kitson looking to be out long term with the knee injury inflicted in the West Brom game, it is worrying in the extreme when Sidibe appears to do a Kitson and seriously damage his knee after just five minutes. He is replaced by Cresswell who looks ineffective in supporting Fuller up front. Fuller looks frustrated and petulant as he picks up his sixth yellow card of the season. Delap's first long throw goes about two yards and it is clear that Delap's now widely reported shoulder injury is also serious. When he gets replaced the lack of strength in depth in our squad is massively exposed. So much so that with twenty minutes left I witness a sight that I never thought I would see, Vincent Pericard making his first Stoke appearance in The Premier League. Are things really that desperate that it has fallen to Pericard to try and win the game?

In truth I cannot remember a credible Stoke chance and Stoke can count themselves fortunate to get a point out of the game. When you consider Fulham were one of the favourites for the drop in pre-season, the relegation alarm bells are now being warmed up. In truth Stoke owe a debt of thanks to Stuart 'goal that wasn't a goal' Atwell for providing pretty much the only entertainment all afternoon. Just after halftime he loses control of the game after some robust tackles fly around. It culminates in a calamitous decision in Stoke's favour. I am sitting seventy five yards away when Danny Higginbotham handballs a Fulham cross in the penalty area. I can see it plain as day. Atwell is about two yards away. It is a shocker and Fulham can feel genuinely aggrieved when Atwell waves play on and then to add insult to injury points to his chest. Perhaps he bottled it in the wake of the vociferous Stoke support or perhaps he is just incompetent. Either way it is a huge let off. The only silver lining to a very grey day is reaching the twenty point mark. Stoke are half way to safety after seventeen games. It is a position we would have taken at the start of the season, but with a worrying drop in form plus suspensions and injuries stretching the squad, the mid-season transfer window cannot come soon enough.

Blackburn Away

There had been much discussion about arranging a drinks party at our house on the Saturday before Christmas. This did not marry well with playing Blackburn away. The problem was easily solved by me volunteering to organise things and then simply not bothering to do it thus rendering the drinks party a non-event. It is through more dishonesty that I find myself a free man on the Saturday before Christmas. With an expected allocation of seven thousand tickets for Stoke fans at Blackburn and the game so close to Christmas, both my brother and I were confident this would not be a sell out. So for the first time this season we were relaxed about the ticket situation for an away game and did not bother to buy tickets from the priority sales. In fact by the time that I had got a green light from home to go, it was well into the general sale period for tickets. I was still relaxed about the ticket situation when I checked Stoke's website, but to my horror found Stoke had sold their entire allocation of four thousand seven hundred tickets. Peter Coates's generous offer to pay for the transport for Stoke's supporters meant a bumper following, but more crucially Greater Manchester Police restricted the ticket allocation for Stoke fans following trouble at games in The North West. It seems a fair few fans got caught short by this.

My brother is pretty unhappy about the news when I break it to him, as he had been waiting on me to get myself organised for this one. He is going to miss out because of my disorganisation. Having arranged every other away ticket this season I only feel partially guilty, but it is still pretty gutting to think we are going to miss out on what looks like being Stoke's biggest away day of the season. With Blackburn rooted to the bottom of The Premier League after a disastrous run of results under Paul Ince, there is genuine belief that this could be our first away win. The only worry is that Paul Ince has been sacked in the week by Blackburn and Sam Allardyce is now in charge. How typical that Stoke could now be facing a resurgent Blackburn after they have suffered six straight defeats and not won at home since September 20th.

It is Saturday lunchtime and I am at home having lunch with the family. Following my failure to organise the drinks party, Kate and I are now planning a night out in London. We have managed to off-load the kids to the in-laws for the evening. I call my brother to ask how I can get the live football streams over the Internet, but he does not answer his phone. He calls me back about 1:30pm. 'What you doing this afternoon?'

'Nothing much, afternoon with Jeff and a live Internet feed if I can get it to work,' I reply, 'then I'm in town with Kate. We're staying up near Holborn.'

'Brilliant, I've found a pub in West Kensington showing the Stoke game live on dodgy satellite. Get yourself on the train. You should just make the kick off.'

'I don't know, I might just quit while I'm ahead otherwise Kate will have to travel into London on her own.' Kate looks up from the paper and gives me a resigned look.

'Go, I'll meet you in Holborn at teatime,' she says. How can I be blessed with such an understanding wife?

Five minutes later and I am speed walking to Reading station. 2:40pm and I arrive at Paddington station. No time for a tube, so I hop into a cab. 'Famous 3 Kings, West Kensington, please mate.'

'Top boozer, going for the football eh? Who do you support then?'

'Stoke.'

'West Ham.'

'Oh yeah, we're at your place next week', I say, not surprised that the cabbie supports West Ham. I call my brother. 'You there yet?'

'Just got here.'

'Busy?'

'Dead.'

'Oh.' I'm disappointed (for no good reason) that a London pub is not packed to the rafters for Stoke v Blackburn, 'I'll be there in 15 minutes.'

Fifteen minutes later, bang on 3pm and with my general knowledge of West Ham's history slightly increased I arrive at a grand looking pub next door to West Kensington tube and I quickly realise this is the arm chair fan's Nirvana. There are four rooms each showing a different live game. There is Fulham v Middlesbrough live in the main front bar, Hull v Sunderland in the function room and Stoke's game at Blackburn is sharing a room with Bolton v Portsmouth. The pub is now filling up fast with exiled London fans following the games on TV. There are a good dozen Stoke shirts on display in our bar and I hook up with my brother and his mate Rowan, who supports Charlton, just as the game kicks off. Rowan is laughing at one of Stoke's players on the TV. 'Pericard's starting?' I ask aghast, looking at the screen.

'The team selection's so strange I can't work out who's playing,' my brother says. It is not helped that our room has the commentary blaring out for the Bolton v Portsmouth game.

'Why no commentary, there's a clear majority of Stoke fans in here?'

'Italian TV feed, so the commentary won't help much.'

Stoke make a bright start, but then a calamitous challenge sees Blackburn's Pederson brought down in the penalty area. Even without commentary we all know it is an obvious penalty. The close up reveals Sonko as the culprit of the mistimed tackle. We still cannot work out the Stoke team even after fifteen minutes. Eventually we think we have got it.

'So we've got three centre backs playing and no right back, three strikers playing in a four four two formation and what is left of our creative players, Soares, Tonge and Pugh all on the bench? Bit harsh on Pugh to be dropped for Cresswell after his performances against Newcastle and Fulham and why is Cresswell playing on the wing? More to the point why is Shawcross playing at right back? This is total madness!' Within half an hour Stoke are 3-0 down to a team that have only scored five at home all season. There is a shot of Sam Allardyce who looks like he cannot quite believe what he is seeing and then another shot of the soaked and dejected Stoke fans in fancy dress. They definitely cannot believe what they are seeing.

I head outside with my brother at halftime. We both agree it is the lowest point of the season so far and considering our next few fixtures, there is real concern about where we will be placed in the league come the end of January. Back in the pub there is anger and disbelief about the team selection amongst our fellow Stoke supporters. They have imploded on the road again and I can barely watch the second half. Stoke recover some composure, but with the game lost it is too little too late and there is going to be no repeat of the Newcastle second half today. Blackburn could have made it four or five by the final whistle and I head off to the tube station to meet Kate feeling utterly dejected, but taking some comfort that I did not actually go to the game.

Man United Home

Boxing Day, the biggest day in the football calendar. Today will see all ninety two league clubs in action, watched live by over half a million football fans. The fixtures computer has been kind to Stoke and it produces the game of the day at The Britannia Stadium. Stoke, who now desperately need to put in a good performance, play Man United, the newly crowned club world champions. Man United are hitting some good form and challenging for the top spot, but they still remain six points behind Liverpool and can ill afford to slip up against Stoke today. Stoke need to hope they can hit Man United on an off day and given Man United's recent return from Japan there is hope that they will be jaded from their trip to The Far East. The game is of course live on Sky and Stoke City will today be exposed to more people than at any other time in their history. The downside to this is an early kick off.

There is never any debate about Boxing Day football in my household and it is pretty much given that it is prioritised over any other event. The only issue today is the early start. Kate will be travelling over to Oxford to see her family in the evening, but she made it clear that she needs the car and she will not be getting up early on Boxing Day. With no train services this causes me a problem getting over to Oxford to meet up with my dad and brother. The only option sees me setting off from Reading at 7:30am on my bike, to ride the twenty five miles over the Chilterns to Oxford. There is not a soul up and it is absolutely freezing. Nearly two hours later I am enjoying a pre-match fry up thanks to my mum. My brother and I then set off on the drive up to Stoke. My dad has opted to watch the game on TV having been ill and not wishing to expose himself to the cold weather.

Early Boxing Day kick offs can occasionally feel a little sombre, but that is not the case today at The Britannia Stadium. It is absolutely rocking inside. There have been suggestions all week that Stoke's fans might be able to bring out the petulant side of Man United with some robust barracking of their superstars. Not for the first time this season I feel a lump at the back of my throat as the teams take to the pitch. Playing Man United at home on Boxing Day. Who would have dared dream about this a year ago when Stoke were at Oakwell? The team selection has also reverted back to the normal four four two after the shambles last week. Injuries see Cresswell partnering Fuller and Pugh back in midfield. A solid defence sees Wilkinson in for Griffin and Shawcross in his favoured central position. Sonko is dropped. Man United show Stoke respect by fielding a full strength side although Ferdinand is not playing after injuring himself in the warm up. Tevez starts with Berbatov on the bench.

Stoke start well and win a couple of long throws, one of which troubles Van Der Sar. The game is tight and perhaps there is a suggestion that Man United are looking jaded, as they create very little. It is obvious that Stoke are well organised and up for the challenge. I am confident from early on that Stoke will give a good account of themselves today. It is half way through the first half when the first real chance falls to Stoke. A neat through ball sees Fuller break clear, but as he is about to shoot, his boot comes off. It is unbelievable. What on earth is going on with Fuller? I head downstairs on forty four minutes to grab the halftime pies and catch Rooney split the Stoke defence on the TV in the concourse. He looks well offside, but scuffs his shot in what is Man United's only clear-cut chance of the half. The replay shows him on side and Stoke can count themselves fortunate to be going in level at halftime.

The second half sees more of the same as Stoke continue to hold Man United. Both sides are limited to half chances and with just twenty five minutes left there is the first real sense that Stoke might get something from the game. Man United sense it as well and the first signs of frustration start to appear. Berbatov is brought on to try and win the game. Neville's barracking of the referee goes up a level. Respect? I don't think so. Rooney swings an elbow in the direction of Abdoulaye Faye and misses. The block ten boys go mental as the referee turns a blind eye to it. Next it is time for the whole of The Brit to go mental as Ronaldo kicks out at Wilkinson after being floored by a brilliant tackle. The Beckham-esque kick is soft, but surely he has to be sent off? Oh it is Man United we are playing so of course the referee takes no action. The game is starting to boil over as the atmosphere reaches fever pitch and it could go either way now.

Wilkinson clatters Ronaldo from behind at knee height. It is beautiful to see as Ronaldo does a 'Platoon'. It is not a nasty challenge, but you can see Wilkinson was stalking Ronaldo for the last few minutes. My brother shows me an immediate text message, 'Wilkinson, love him!' It is from an Everton fan. It is no doubt a booking, but a yellow card at most. The bloke next to me says 'That's Wilkinson gone along with any chance of winning this game.' Of course he has already been booked, so he will be off. It is a shame to be sent off for something so daft especially as Wilkinson has had a great game. He walks off to a standing ovation from the Stoke fans and has to suffer the humiliation of the waving from the two and half thousand Man United fans by the tunnel. Twenty minutes to survive for a point.

With just ten men the Man United winner is inevitable. It comes with ten minutes remaining from Tevez turning in a miss-hit shot from Berbatov. It is a bit harsh, but at least it was not in injury time and ultimately it is Stoke's own indiscipline that has cost them. It is massive for Man United and you can see the relief from the Man United bench and their fans. Win ugly and you win the league. Today was the perfect example of why Man United will probably win the league.

Due to the early kick off we listen to all the other games on Radio 5 on the way home. All the results go against Stoke and they plummet four places down the table and back into the relegation zone. It is a Boxing Day to wipe from the memory, but when I am out in the local pub in Oxford with my brother later that evening there is a general consensus from the Oxfordshire armchair reds that Stoke gave Man United a right good scare today. Just the fact we are even discussing the game at length in an Oxfordshire pub is a reminder of where Stoke are. I cannot remember discussing our 3-3 draw with Barnsley in the pub this time last year.

West Ham Away

The last game of 2008 and the first game of the second half of the season, sees the first of five games in London. Even with twenty points Stoke are still in the relegation zone and this suggests that forty points might not be enough to survive come the end of the season. The only positive is that Stoke are one of fourteen teams genuinely locked in the relegation battle. It is the closest Premier League ever and just seven points separate seventh place in the table from the relegation zone. There are also a number of teams in crisis. Middlesbrough and Hull both have worse form records than Stoke. Spurs' post Redknapp bounce is long gone and they are once again staring into the abyss. Perhaps most interesting though is West Ham. They are a team in financial crisis and there is likely to be a fire sale in the transfer window. There are rumours they may not even make it to the end of season without going into administration and their current form is shocking, just one win in eleven going into Boxing Day. I would have fancied this today had West Ham not just thrashed Portsmouth, another crisis club, 4-1 at Fratton Park.

Having stayed over in Oxford for the last couple of nights after Boxing Day, my brother and I are making our way to Upton Park from Oxford. It is an early start when we board the coach from Oxford to London. It may be a London game, but Upton Park is a nightmare to get to, especially on a Sunday with large parts of The Underground closed off for engineering works and especially because we have to go via my brother's flat in Hammersmith. In the end it takes nearly three hours door to door and we arrive at the main reception of Upton

Park at 12:30pm.

My brother has a mate, Tom, who is the Opta consultant for West Ham and we have had it on good authority that he might be able to get us into the players lounge for some pre-match drinks. We are met and get a couple of free programmes, but rather than being allowed inside Upton Park we are instead taken to The Boleyn Tavern, which very clearly positions itself as a pub only for home fans. It is packed to the rafters with Grant Mitchell look-alikes and I am pretty grateful that Tom is wearing his full West Ham tracksuit. There is a genuine atmosphere of menace in here and Tom takes great pleasure in telling us that we would probably get a good battering if we were identified as Stoke supporters. I had already worked that out for myself. Tom has the best job of anyone I have ever met. He compiles all the Opta stats and briefs West Ham's management and playing staff with post-match and pre-match analysis. As such he has had to watch recordings of Stoke's previous five league games and his knowledge on Stoke's players and tactics is phenomenal. He leaves after a pint to take part in the West Ham pre-match team brief and we arrange to meet after the game. My brother and I are left to fend for ourselves in what is probably the most intimidating pub I have ever been in. We watch Livepool thrash our relegation rivals Newcastle 5-1 at St James' Park. When inevitably the DJ puts on 'I'm forever blowing bubbles' we are the only ones in the whole pub not singing. We are clocked and it is definitely time to leave. It ends up being a long walk around the backstreets to the away turnstiles and we get in the ground pretty much on 2pm as the game is kicking off. I am now well up for it and expect some proper cockney banter from the West Ham boys this afternoon. It is great to be back on the road again with Stoke City.

It is not a bad Stoke following, but not a sell-out. The journey length coupled with the early kick off appears to have dampened the away spirit, as it is a bit quieter than normal. Perhaps it is the aftermath of the Blackburn away disaster and the fact we have not scored for three games that is leaving people a bit sombre. Fuller is looking more and more petulant every game and rumours abound that Everton are lining up a bid for him in the transfer window. With Kitson and Sidibe looking like being out long term I am wondering where our goals will come from. The answer comes very quickly at Upton Park. Pugh delivers Stoke's first corner and it is met with a bullet header from Abdoulaye Faye. Stoke are 1-0 up in just four minutes. The celebration is of course wild and the West Ham fans to our left, who seem more intent on taunting us than watching the game, are left looking stunned. The relegation taunt to West Ham is immediate. It is the first time Stoke have led away from home all season. Stoke sit back and West Ham attack for most of the next forty minutes. Stoke have a couple of half chances to make it 2-0, but everyone is more than happy to be leading away from home at halftime.

In the concourse, my brother and I celebrate the rare and happy feeling of leading away from home. We also tempt fate by discussing how a win today will see Stoke springboard up the table and out of the relegation zone. Three points could see Stoke move up seven places in the table today. Just five minutes into the second half and I am cursing the tempting of fate at halftime. Another two minutes later and we witness one of the worst moments I have ever seen as a Stoke fan. There is no real complaint about West Ham's equaliser. Although it is disappointing, it was always coming. However the aftermath to the goal sees Cresswell, Fuller and Griffin squaring off in the middle of the pitch. I miss the initial incident, but next thing we know Fuller's been given a straight red and there is not a West Ham player anywhere near the incident. Most people appear as baffled as me, but some are suggesting that Fuller and Griffin raised arms at each other with Cresswell acting as peacemaker. Not surprisingly there is no replay of the incident on the big screen so my brother calls Tom to see if he has access to Opta feeds.

Whether what Tom tells us is one hundred percent

accurate we cannot be sure, but his take is that Fuller had a go at Griffin after he failed to deal with a clearance that led to the goal. Then Griffin walked half the length of the pitch to retaliate to Fuller as the game was about to re-start. Cresswell is confirmed as peacemaker, but Fuller slaps Griffin after words are exchanged. The referee gets involved and Tom tells us Griffin is seen clearly telling the referee to send Fuller off. Ultimately we will probably never know the full story, but it is a shocking display of ill discipline from both players that will cost Stoke today. Perhaps more worrying is that the incident exposes a lack of team cohesion and dressing room spirit at a time in the season when it is required the most.

The rest of the game feels like a non-event after this and I feel sure West Ham will go on to win the game. Stoke consolidate well and defend resolutely without seriously threatening West Ham. Still feeling let down by the Griffin / Fuller incident I struggle to get behind the team and feel it is only a matter of time. Ultimately West Ham hit Stoke very late, just when I am starting to think a point has been saved from a hopeless situation of Stoke's own making. It is an eighty eighth minute winner from a cruel deflection and has a very strong suspicion of offside. We have to endure the taunts of The Hammers fans. They have not been as vocal as on previous visits to Upton Park, but they have enjoyed their day. Stoke appear to have hit rock bottom.

I feel so down as I walk back towards Upton Park tube station. We have arranged to meet Tom in The Duke Of Edinburgh pub. It is another huge West Ham pub that is full of menace. The Grant Mitchell appreciation society has obviously decided to move on from The Boleyn Arms to come and taunt any Stoke fans about what we have all just witnessed. Fortunately their lads are now in joyous mood following back to back wins as West Ham now find themselves in the top half of the table. Stoke meanwhile have to thank Robinho for maintaining their league position as we watch Man City peg back Blackburn in the late live game. It is a bleak day for

Blackburn as they throw away the lead after being 2-0 with two minutes left. With West Brom beating Spurs and Stoke facing Liverpool and Chelsea next, I am pretty sure Stoke will be adrift at the bottom of the table by the end of January.

Hartlepool Away

'The big day has arrived!' My opening line to Kate this morning was greeted with a smile. 'FA Cup third round day, don't you just love it?' The smile is gone. It is of course Kate's sister's wedding. It may have been months in the planning, but they still managed to clash with a football day. Initially I thought Jon and Susannah (well Jon anyway) had arranged their wedding around the football fixtures, but of course Saturday January 3rd was left blank to accommodate the FA Cup. To be honest the FA Cup is pretty much always a non-event for Stoke City fans, with Stoke not having gone beyond the last sixteen since the early seventies and having suffered plenty of humiliation in that time. However, when the third round draw was made there was still the usual anticipation. I figured that if Stoke were involved in a big clash then the game might get moved to the Sunday anyway. When Stoke's ball was drawn away to Hartlepool that scenario seemed unlikely and it was never going to be a game where I would risk the wrath of Kate to attend.

As it happens the game is an early kick off and this means the second half clashes with the church service. In truth I can see huge advantages both for the club and for me personally if Hartlepool put one over us today. Pulis selects a much weakened side, but one that should still be strong enough to progress. Andrew Davies makes his Stoke debut after being signed in the summer and then being injured all season. Kitson is back on the bench. I am strictly on family wedding duty today. This means no drinking, plenty of driving and keeping my daughters in line as the bridesmaids. I get an opportunity just before the service starts to grab the halftime score on Radio 5 from the wedding car I am driving. 0-0 and the suggestion that a cup upset is on the cards against a poor looking Stoke side is not what I want to hear.

I am sitting in a side pew at the front of the church, next to Kate and in full gaze of the family. There is going to be no opportunity to follow the game on my phone here. It is only when the signing of the registers happens and Kate disappears off up the front of the church that I can check the scores. I cannot get a proper phone signal in the middle of rural Oxfordshire and it takes ages for my phone to connect. The phone is returned to my inside suit pocket. I turn my attention to failing to control my two daughters, who by now are getting pretty bored and have started the destruction of their bouquets.

Kate returns and we exit the church. My parents are outside. They did not attend the service, but have come to see the wedding procession. My dad looks like he is at a funeral rather than a wedding and I immediately know why. The eye contact and shake of the head is a clear sign that once my post wedding service duties are complete, I will be having the 'at least we can concentrate on the league' conversation with him. Jon's dad grabs me during the photos. He supports Wolves. '2-0 to Hartlepool, what a humiliation', he says with glee.

'It's not the end of the world,' I say, 'at least we can concentrate on the league.' I head over to my dad.

'Another to add to the Blyth Spartans, Nuneaton Borough and Telford United humiliations', he says.

'It's not the end of the world,' I say, 'at least we can concentrate on the league.'

In truth I am really not that worried and I put the whole sorry story of this year's FA Cup to the back of my mind as I drive some of the wedding party over to the reception in central Oxford. During a season of mid-table mediocrity, the cup exit usually signals the end of the season. However, this year the cliché of concentrating on the league has real meaning and it also frees up plenty of Saturdays in January and February. Jon grabs me at the reception. 'Congratulations', I say.

'Thanks, what was the score today?' he replies.

'Like you don't know.'

'At least you can concentrate on the league. Anyway one of my mates supports Vale and he's keen to meet you.'

'I bet he is', I say making a mental note to avoid anyone who looks like they are from Burslem for the rest of the day.

Truth be told, it is not a great day for me. I cannot drink because I am driving and I am obliged to make small talk with people who are getting increasingly drunk as the evening wears on. Everyone seems to be taking great pleasure in Stoke getting knocked out of the cup by Hartlepool. There are people who I do not even know coming up to me for a bit of Hartlepool banter. It is about 10:30pm when I clock him heading across the dance floor. That has to be a Burslem beer gut heading my way. He is fat, he is drunk, he has got his Becks bottle on the dance floor, but the real give away is the rather simple look to him. He is a Vale fan for sure. 'So you're the Stoke boy?' he slurs. We exchange pleasantries and I explain my connections to Stoke-on-Trent.

'I take it you're from Burslem then?'

'Yep, but Vale are only my second team. I really support Man United.' This has to be a wind up. I look for Jon to see if this is some sort of joke to get things spiced up at the wedding reception. 'Stoke in The Premier League. What a complete joke. Whatever next?'

'Dunno, Vale in The Conference?' I am getting to the point where a few car park handbags might be inevitable here.

'Anyway what about Hartlepool then?'

'At least we can concentrate on the league,' I say offering a handshake to close the conversation, knowing that this is not the time or place to try and settle any Stoke Vale rivalry.

Liverpool Home

Last night I went to The Madejski Stadium. It was last season that I introduced my eldest daughter to the beautiful game. I was a bit surprised when she seemed to get rather hooked on the experience and I ended up taking her to a couple of Premier League games involving Reading. I have been pestered all season to take her to see Reading again and last night's Friday evening kick off represented pretty much the only opportunity to avoid a clash with a Stoke game. I wish Reading well as my local team, but I really struggle with it. With the exception of one small block of lads, The Madejski Stadium is like a morgue even when there are twenty thousand plus inside. It is always a bad sign when the PA blares out a tune when a goal is scored and last night it happened four times as Reading spanked Watford 4-0. Ellie now insists she is a Reading fan and absolutely refuses to come and watch Stoke play. It will be interesting next season if Stoke survive and Reading bounce back. Maybe Kate will be taking Ellie in the home end while my brother and I sit with the Stoke boys.

The sterile Madejski experience left me craving for The Britannia and today it is back to the reality of Premier League survival for Stoke. There is no huge expectation of a points fest in January, but it is important Stoke stay in touch with seventeenth place in the table. This will mean it is not a lost cause once they get to the more winnable games in February and March. Today sees the last of 'The Big Four' games at home. Liverpool remain top of the league, but are under mounting pressure from Chelsea and Man United. Stoke have bought Etherington from West Ham in the transfer window. This has generated much excitement, as Etherington is known as being a creative, wide player. Lawrence and Kitson are both back from injury. The squad is starting to regain its strength. With Fuller suspended and Sidibe still injured, Cresswell partners Kitson up front. Wilkinson is also back after suspension and joins Higginbotham, Abdoulaye Faye and Shawcross in what now looks to be Stoke's strongest defensive line-up.

For weeks there had been a question mark over me attending the Liverpool home game as we had been invited to a thirtieth birthday celebration in Reading on the Saturday evening. With the game then re-scheduled to kick off at 5:30pm for a live Setanta broadcast, I thought I might have to miss this one. Having leveraged my good behaviour at the wedding I find myself on the 2:00pm train heading from Reading to Oxford. The later start makes a nice change from the usual Saturday morning rush and I meet my brother at Oxford station for the drive up the M6. My dad is still not well and opts to watch the game on Setanta. We had planned to meet Scouse Phil and his mates before the game, but on hearing they've been on the lash in Crewe since 11am and knowing neutral drinking options close to The Brit do not exist, we decide to give it a wide birth. The early arrival at The Brit leaves plenty of time to watch the afternoon's results come in on Soccer Saturday. In an act of generosity, my brother also reveals that he is happy to drive me back to Reading so that I can minimise being late for the party later.

The pre-match atmosphere is right up there again as the teams enter the field. Liverpool's line-up is strong, but Keane, Babel and Torres are all on the bench for a game Liverpool must win to keep the pressure on at the top of the league. It is immediately obvious that it will be Gerrard that gets the brunt of the abuse from Stoke's fans today. This is fuelled by Gerrard's Christmas run in with the law, after the now infamous Southport nightclub incident. Stoke are up for it today and go at Liverpool from the off, with new boy Etherington making an immediate impact. Delap fires in the first long throw and it is clear his shoulder is now better as it causes pandemonium following a poor Liverpool clearance. A cross finds Abdoulaye Faye, who heads it back to Delap who now must score himself. Delap's shot is cracked against the post and the rebound falls to Cresswell who has an open goal. Cresswell does not react in time and the chance falls wide. It seems Cresswell is destined not to score in The Premier League.

Stoke limit Liverpool to half chances, with a couple of good saves from Sorenson keeping Liverpool at bay. Meanwhile Stoke continue to apply pressure and cause Liverpool problems. I feel a goal for Stoke is coming. Etherington puts in a great cross that finds Shawcross in the clear and he comfortably heads the ball past Reina into the back of the net. I am in full celebration mode, not looking at the pitch, just going crazy. My brother grabs me, 'It's off-side!' I regain my senses and to my embarrassment I find I am pretty much the only one celebrating a clearly offside goal. 'You looked like a right cock.' my brother informs me. My embarrassment is short lived as one of the best first half performances of the season by Stoke sees the scores level at halftime, with Stoke unfortunate not to be in the lead.

I enjoy halftime reflecting on a good performance with Stoke looking like they can take something from this game. It is a fabulous response to the calamities at West Ham and Hartlepool. Liverpool come out for the second half fired up, but within five minutes a miss-kick from Reina lands at the feet of Kitson with no defender near him. He reacts well, takes the ball round Reina and although the angle is tight he must score. The shot ends up in the side netting. Like Cresswell, Kitson looks destined never to score for Stoke in The Premier League. How we miss Fuller and Sidibe. How we need to get a decent striker in the transfer window.

Liverpool are starting to panic and Babel and Torres are on for the last fifteen minutes. The opportunity for three points may have escaped us, but Stoke deserve a draw at the very least as we enter the Liverpool kill zone. Ten minutes left and Stoke win a free kick in prime Whelan territory, but frenzied activity on the touchline sees the return of Lawrence to The Premier League for the first time in four months. The noise that greets Lawrence is raucous. Is it his destiny to win the game with his first touch? Whelan's having none of it and strikes a brilliant free kick. With Reina well beaten the ball curls agonisingly wide and brushes the outside of the post. Half the ground thinks it is in. Perhaps instead we are destined to witness the full cruelty of a late Liverpool winner. The warning sign comes on eighty four minutes when a Gerrard free kick hits the bar. The tension now is unbearable as Liverpool go for the winner and Stoke try and hold out for a point.

Stoke attempt to slow down a frenzied Liverpool with a late substitution. Pugh on for Kitson. Three minutes of injury time. Liverpool go direct. Torres finds Gerrard, who turns and shoots from distance. Sorenson is beaten and the ball is heading for the corner of the goal. So cruel, so typical, so Liverpool. It seems Gerrard will make us pay today for the barracking he has received. Almost in slow motion the ball hits the post and goes out for a goal kick. Gerrard looks distraught, as the last chance to win the game is so agonisingly close for Liverpool. The referee blows and it is a vital point for Stoke and two huge lost points for Liverpool. Liverpool have now dropped four points against Stoke. How important will that be at the end of the season? Possibly not as important as the two points Stoke have secured from Liverpool in their relegation battle.

Confident Man United fans dominate the journey home on 606. Stoke have had a huge impact on the destiny of the Premier League title and Liverpool's failure today is a massive boost in Man United's preparation for their Super Sunday showdown with Chelsea. My brother drives me back and I am in Reading by 10:15pm. Kate's fine and drinking with the girls so I head to the bar to chat footy with the lads. I get a Stella thrust into my hand. 'It's a thank you present', says Manc Paul, a genuine Man United fan I know in Reading, 'we owe Stoke big time for the favour this season.' I accept the pint, but am less than comfortable with the idea that Stoke have handed Man United the league title this season. Match Of The Day comes on in the pub and I witness again how close Gerrard was to spoiling our day.

Chelsea Away

For me Chelsea away is the game I have been relishing most since we got promoted. I know loads of Chelsea glory hunters where I live, so even though there is zero expectation of getting a result at Stamford Bridge today, I have enjoyed baiting the local Chelsea fans with suggestions of reversible Arsenal shirts and threadbare armchairs. With the exception of Fulham away, this is the shortest journey I will make to watch Stoke this season. Stamford Bridge is just a short distance from my brother's flat. The price of the extortionate match tickets is offset by negligible transport costs as I make the short trip into West London.

I meet my brother in Putney at midday in what can best be described as a posh footy pub. There are plenty of Chelsea shirts on show even though it is early, but the pub is not crowded and we get seats in big leather armchairs by the fireplace. There is a gastro pub feel to the place, but there are still plasma screens and free newspapers to get us in the mood for the game. It is the perfect pre-match scene for Chelsea away and the excitement is tangible. The reason we met south of the river is because we have hooked up with George, an old mate from Reading, who supports Rangers and now lives in Southfields. Rangers George had been keen to come to the game and given we had not sold our away allocation for West Ham, I thought it might be possible to get George a ticket during the general sale period. As it happens though Stoke have only taken an allocation of nineteen hundred for the game. Whilst I can understand the commercial position, given what happened at West Ham, this is surprising and a bit disappointing. George shares the news that he is to become a dad in July and he is still reeling from this life changing news. So when we get to 2:30pm, George heads off pram shopping for the afternoon, while my brother and I head for East Putney tube station.

I was last at Stamford Bridge nearly fifteen years ago when Stoke dumped Chelsea out of The League Cup in the second round. It was a glorious night with Pesci scoring the only goal. Stamford Bridge was pretty much derelict then and what greets us as we exit Fulham Broadway is unrecognisable from that night. Stamford Bridge and the surrounding area have been transformed and it is now a magnificent stadium. We enter the stadium at 2:45pm able to accept in good spirits the inevitable spanking Stoke are about to receive. The smaller than expected Stoke following is in excellent voice even though we are split over two tiers. Some of the Chelsea boys are up for it, particularly those behind the goals, but I am struck once again by the corporate and sterile feel to the place. It was not like this last time I was here. Then it was seriously intimidating. I take my seat five rows back in the top tier.

Stoke field the same team as last week with one very notable exception. Since the Liverpool game Stoke have signed James Beattie from Sheffield United in what looks like a very good piece of business. In Beattie Stoke have now got a proven Premier League goal scorer. The only surprise is that Pulis has dropped Kitson rather than Cresswell, effectively pushing Kitson to fourth choice once Fuller and Sidibe return. Stoke provide an immediate scare as Chelsea fail to deal with a Delap long throw in the first minute. Chelsea's home form has been questionable this season and there does appear to be a lack of creativity again today. The home fans are notably restless for a comprehensive victory as they see Chelsea dominate possession. It is only through some desperate defending and brilliant goal keeping from Sorenson that the score remains 0-0 at halftime.

The concourse atmosphere is buzzing and we are able to revel in frustrating Chelsea. Stoke start the second half strongly and create some good half chances, most notably when Beattie punts a long lob just over the bar, with Cech struggling to get back. Half an hour left and the first thoughts of points spring to mind, especially when Ballack heads wide when it looks easier to score. Maybe, just maybe we have caught Chelsea on an off day and we will get that bit of luck needed to secure a first away win. A long ball finds Beattie, who neatly turns and slots the ball to Delap. Delap controls the ball at pace and holds off Chelsea's defenders. It is hard to see because it is at the far end of the ground, but there is enough time for me to think that Delap has a great chance to score. Delap coolly chips the ball over Cech and into the back of the net for a brilliant goal. Then it is bedlam, absolute bedlam. I am at the front of the tier, five rows down from my seat. I do not even remember running down the steps. The guy next to me is stood on the wall, arms aloft with a thirty foot drop to the tier below. Everyone is going mental in front of a stunned Stamford Bridge. I have no idea how long the celebration lasts, but it is up there with the best I have experienced with Stoke. A steward grabs my shoulders and tells me to get back to my seat or I will be ejected from the stadium. Given that I am about to pass out anyway, it is not a problem and I return to my brother. The game is well underway again and the clock shows Stoke have to hold on for twenty five minutes to record the biggest shock of The Premier League season so far and destroy any chance Chelsea have of winning the league.

Stamford Bridge is stunned, their players are in panic and Scolari looks like a dead man walking. Defeat here will surely see him sacked. Lampard leads the Chelsea cause and Stoke have to defend deep. Lampard spurns chances and takes the brunt of the abuse from the Stoke fans in his stride. There is no Ronaldo style petulance on display today from Chelsea. Ten minutes left and although Chelsea have had enough possession and spurned many chances to win the game, there is an increasing sense that today will be Stoke's day. Scolari is being taunted about his job and some of the Chelsea fans are joining in. Stamford Bridge is beginning to empty and it is not just a handful, hundreds are leaving. Scolari uses the last of his subs to try and exploit the wings and save his job. Stoke's defence is now all over the place. A couple of dangerous crosses are just about dealt with and a quick look at the scoreboard shows eighty eight minutes played. There have been no injuries, so it is so close now. Another wide move sees a deep cross and head back across goal. Sorenson's caught in no man's land and Belletti sneaks in the equaliser just inside the post.

Of course it is disappointing to be hit so late, but a draw is no good for Chelsea and the muted celebrations suggest there is not enough time to win the game. Stoke will leave with a vital point and the moral victory today. Ninety minutes played and the game is surely over. The fourth official holds up his board and I am expecting one, maybe two minutes. The board shows four minutes and there is a huge cheer around Stamford Bridge. Nobody expected that and now there is real danger as Chelsea press for the winner. It is desperate and I cannot bear to watch. There are three minutes of frenzied goalmouth action as crosses rain in from the flanks. I remain convinced Stoke will survive as the defence deals with the danger. The whistles from the Stoke fans are now deafening. Another cross comes in and is not cleared. The ball drops to Lampard on the edge of the penalty area and he blasts it through the crowd of Stoke defenders who are desperately trying to make the vital block. The world stops as the ball hits the back of the net. It is the single most sickening moment I have experienced as a Stoke fan. I sink to the steps, head in hands as the adrenaline drains from me. A now frenzied Stamford Bridge feels utterly surreal. I do not feel emotional, I just feel sick. This is the defining moment when relegation becomes a reality and I am not mentally prepared for the dramatic circumstances in which Chelsea have so cruelly hammered that realisation home.

Spurs Away

My brother and I had left Stamford Bridge in a state of shock. We had wandered the streets unable to speak for a while. Eventually we found our way to a quiet pub just off the Kings Road. It did not stay quiet for long and was soon full of Chelsea fans in buoyant mood. We left and found another pub near Parsons Green where we could start the process of healing from such a traumatic end to the game. The combination of such a high octane adrenalin buzz from Delap's goal and then the utter deflation of losing the game so late left me feeling down for several days. Never has a football result had such a profound and long lasting affect on my wellbeing. It took until Wednesday for me to really snap out of it. Watching Spurs beat Burnley in The League Cup semi final on TV was the catalyst for my own post Chelsea recovery. Burnley had clawed back a three goal deficit at home in the second leg and were ninety seconds from Wembley when Spurs cruelly dumped them out of the cup. Burnley's fans experienced something even crueller than we had against Chelsea and it was great therapy for me to realise there is always somebody worse off than you.

Despite the cup win, that analogy could be applied to tonight's opponents Spurs in terms of the league. With West Brom picking up points over Christmas, Spurs once again found themselves rooted to the foot of the table after we had played Chelsea. Only a draw at home in the Sunday match against relegation threatened Portsmouth, saw them lift above Stoke on goal difference. Tonight's evening kick off at White Hart Lane is a relegation six pointer if ever there was one.

Of all the away games to fall on an evening, it is probably

most disappointing for me that it is Spurs. Like Upton Park, White Hart Lane is a difficult ground to get to and there is little time between finishing work and the 8pm kick off for any pre-match socialising. One of my regular drinking partners from Reading, Chris, is a big Spurs fan and he had promised to take me to White Hart Lane when we secured promotion. Chris and I meet in Paddington and get the tube over to Liverpool Street where we are also meeting my brother, Rangers George and another friend called Richard, who supports Celtic. The tube ends up delaying us and we do not get to the pub on Liverpool Street station until 7pm. I had originally hoped to meet up around 5pm, but everyone's work commitments made that pretty much impossible. It is then that I find out my brother has cried off the game because of some mysterious foot injury. He has been off work all week and cannot actually walk. Chris and I meet Rangers George and Celtic Richard and as a result of trying to squeeze in a round of drinks we miss the 7:20pm train to White Hart Lane. The next one is 7:30pm, arriving at 7:51pm and so it is now going to be a quick dash to make the kick off. The evening is turning into a bit of a rushed shambles.

Our train stops just outside Stamford Hill and does not move. I get a text from a Spurs supporting colleague telling me that the Stoke boys are making loads of noise and asking whether I am there. Our train arrives ten minutes late and it is well past 8pm as I run up the stairs to my seat in the second tier. Chris and George have gone in the home end. Richard has flogged his home ticket on the street and decided to take my brother's away ticket, so he is running up the stairs after me. There is a huge roar and it is immediately obvious we have missed a goal. As I enter the stadium, the now silent and glum faced Stoke fans tell me it is 1-0 to Spurs with ten minutes played. We find our seats and I try and work out the team whilst taking in a spectacular White Hart Lane. There is now a full on atmosphere throughout an away ground for the first time this season. Respect to the Spurs fans for that. Almost immediately Spurs score a second and four minutes later the game is over as Bentley has a clear header for the third.

Stoke, like my brother, have not turned up. It is a carbon copy of the Blackburn game except this time Spurs are rampant and an absolute thrashing is on the cards. At halftime 3-0 is generous to Stoke. It really could have been five or six. I remain in my seat and the inquest begins. Cresswell has been favoured over Fuller and there is harsh criticism again of the team selection and tactics. Against the quality players Spurs have at their disposal, the tactic to standoff and play deep has proved to be suicidal. It is a desperately depressing scene and for the first time this season there is vocal criticism of Pulis in the away end at halftime.

A change is made just after halftime with Fuller replacing Amdy Faye. Stoke now have an outlet and they suddenly look dangerous, but there is a mountain to climb. With half an hour left Etherington puts Beattie through and Beattie finds a quality finish to make it 3-1. It is Beattie's first goal for Stoke and the technique and confidence of the finish is a positive sign. It all feels a little bit too little too late for this game, but it does spark life into Stoke's fans. The atmosphere around White Hart Lane is fabulous for the last half an hour. Spurs look nervous as Stoke dominate after Beattie's goal. A second Stoke goal now would set up a barnstorming finish. The chance arrives on eighty five minutes when Etherington whips in a perfect cross to an unmarked Cresswell, but he heads the ball wide from four yards. The game fizzles out and we have to endure the taunts of 'going down' from the home fans. When I meet Chris, he like all the Spurs fans, is delighted with the performance and the result. The result eases Spurs' relegation concerns. Stoke are now nineteenth. Only West Brom's 5-0 defeat, at home by Man United, keeps Stoke off the bottom of the table.

Man City Home

How can you have any realistic expectation of winning a game when the opposition have spent ten times more money assembling their side? In the case of Man City their total spend is now well in excess of one hundred million pounds after their mid-season spending spree and even that ended up being modest compared to their aspirations for this period. Today could have seen the debut of Kaka for Man City at The Britannia Stadium, but as Man City are quickly discovering even obscene amounts of money cannot buy you instant success. The beauty of being a football fan is that even when all the odds are stacked against your team, pre-match you always have hope. This is how I feel today on the early journey north. My brother is away somewhere for the weekend so I am travelling to the game with just my dad. I suspect he may have preferred to watch the game on Sky, but as he has only attended one game in person in the last two months he did not take too much persuading today. With huge engineering works on the line between Reading and Oxford this weekend and an early kick off, I have to leave my house at 8:30am and get picked up from Didcot at 9:45am.

Stoke are now desperate for points. Assuming they do not get a result against Man City today, there are still enough winnable games to survive against relegation, but it really is starting to look bleak. Stoke have gone eleven games, in all competitions, without a win and we really should be considering them a club in crisis. It is a positive thing that we are not and the truth is Stoke are not in crisis, well not yet anyway. Three tough London away games mixed in with

Man United and Liverpool at home was never going to yield many points and even if Stoke lose today they will probably still be in touch with seventeenth place in the table. It is interesting though that the media have regularly cited West Brom, Middlesbrough, Hull, Newcastle, Portsmouth, Spurs and Sunderland as being 'crisis clubs' and yet Stoke are never mentioned. I suspect this is because everyone outside Stoke-on-Trent wrote off Stoke City before a ball was even kicked this season.

Man City at home is a huge game. It almost feels like a local derby. Last time they visited both Stoke and Man City were relegated to the third tier of English football on a day that saw chaos and violence at The Britannia Stadium. There will be no repeat of those scenes today with organised security and proper ticket allocation, but there is still a tension in the air pre-match. Man City have been abysmal on the road this season and that gives us hope. There is also a big question mark over Robinho. On some occasions he looks exceptional, but on others he looks plain ordinary. Will he and the other Man City mercenaries fancy a freezing and hostile Britannia Stadium today? Robinho will be today's target for The Boothen End, primarily because of his high profile, but also because of his recent and highly publicised brush with the law. The game kicks off and it does indeed feel hostile in The Brit today.

Fuller is back in the starting line-up and partners Beattie for the first time. The only other change sees Pugh replace an injured Higginbotham at the back. Lawrence continues to start from the bench, but in truth it is difficult to see where he would fit into the team today. Stoke defend deep and even with the pace that Man City have, they initially have trouble breaking Stoke down. Just as Stoke look like they are starting to get on top in the game, Wright-Phillips splits the Stoke defence with a blinding counter attack. The cross finds Robinho unmarked in the middle and he has to score. Instead Robinho, who has looked disinterested so far, scuffs a weak shot straight at Sorenson. I can clearly remember when Man

City bought Robinho someone in the media raised the point that Robinho's true worth would not be based on how he performs at Eastlands in the glorious August sunshine, but how he performs at The Britannia Stadium in the middle of winter. Every Man City fan now knows the answer and Hughes must fear the dreadful lack of spirit his mega signing is showing this afternoon in the face of The Britannia challenge.

On thirty seven minutes one single incident over shadows everything in the first half. I get a confused view, but what I see is Wright-Phillips go in high and two footed on Etherington who is left motionless on the floor. Delap steams in, retaliates with a trip on Wright-Phillips and then another follow-up tackle. The Seddon Stand boys who have a full view of the incident are going berserk and then it is hand bags all round as a number of Man City and Stoke players get involved in scuffles. Inevitably someone is going to get sent off in the aftermath and the two obvious candidates are Delap and Wright-Phillips. Incredibly no action is taken against Wright-Phillips and Delap gets a straight red. It is game over surely?

The noise that follows the incident is truly incredible. The Britannia Stadium is louder and more hostile than it has ever been before. I have never witnessed noise like it anywhere at a football ground. The full wrath is aimed at the referee and Wright-Phillips. Much has been written in recent weeks about whether a crowd can genuinely influence the outcome of a game and many people are suggesting it is the single most important factor that accounts for the difference between Stoke's home form and their away form. Personally I have always been sceptical about this and believe the crowd makes only a negligible difference at most. Today is the day when my scepticism is eradicated. It is clear the noise from Stoke's fans lifts the players. More importantly, it is also clear to see Man City's players are intimidated, appear confused by Stoke's tactics and are frightened to take risks going forward. A number of marginal decisions go Stoke's way as Man City's fans are silenced. They must be struggling to comprehend how a side of such individual talent, looks completely unable to break down the league's supposed whipping boys now that they only have ten men.

Five minutes of injury time are signalled and it is right in the fifth minute that Etherington breaks clear. His cross finds Beattie, who brilliantly twists back to drop off his marker and find a yard of space. His clear header is planted firmly in the bottom corner and The Britannia Stadium erupts. The goal comes unexpectedly, but it is perfectly timed to hurt Man City. The halftime whistle blows immediately and there is a rush to get into the concourse to see the halftime highlights on Sky and make sense of the Delap sending off. The replays are reasonably conclusive. Wright-Phillips' tackle on Etherington has the potential to be a career ender, but it is perfectly timed. Had it been the other way round it would have had the Stoke fans on their feet applauding. Delap overreacts and has kicked the ball at Wright-Phillips while he was on the ground from his initial foul. There can be little argument about his red card. However Wright-Phillips has kicked out viciously at Delap, sparking the wider scuffle. The referee has either made a terrible misjudgement or missed it. Either way Wright-Phillips should have been sent off and there is real injustice that Stoke are a man down.

As the second half kicks off everyone in the stadium now knows what has happened and the anger is pure. The referee will experience a difficult second half. Fuller has looked poor and is sacrificed with Cresswell as Stoke go into a four four one formation. It is hard to fathom why Cresswell is used rather than Lawrence and you have to start to wonder if the conspiracy theories about Lawrence joining a Championship side in the transfer window might be true. Stoke park the bus in front of their goal and Man City will have to do something creative to break Stoke down. The game forms into a pattern where Man City totally dominate possession. However every Stoke player is heroic as they are roared on by the fanatical home support. Man City cannot get within twenty yards of

Stoke's goal as their fans stand in silent disbelief at what they are witnessing. It should be totally nerve wracking as Stoke close in for their first win over two months, but it is not. Stoke close out Man City so effectively and Man City display such a lack of invention that Stoke seem to comfortably weather the storm.

With five minutes left I do start to fear the worst, especially with the Chelsea experience still raw. Man City finally break clear and substitute Griffin brings down Richards in the box. There is a huge appeal from the Man City players and their fans. I feel sure a penalty will be given, but incredibly it is dismissed. We can give the referee the benefit of the doubt in terms of how he interpreted it, but frankly I think he bottled it. Ultimately I think the crowd today affected that decision. What I saw was a penalty and replays will ultimately confirm that to be the case. When the game finishes you can sense the relief around The Britannia. It is another joyous moment. The questionable penalty decision should take nothing away from what is a heroic Stoke performance and a massive three points. This is the biggest win of the season so far as it brings Stoke back from the brink and out of the relegation zone for the first time since Boxing Day.

Walking back to the car park I cross the path of four Manc lads and one of them takes a step towards me. I do not quite catch what he says, but it is all pretty nasty. I turn the other cheek. No point in spoiling a good win with some facial damage, but my reaction is actually one of pity more than anything. I have no gripe with Man City fans. They have suffered, done their time more than most and today they have experienced the ultimate humiliation. The gloating with Arab headdresses and wads of cash is now a distant memory. The reality of their new venture is getting turned over by ten man Stoke. Last season, without their money this sort of result would have gone largely unnoticed. However coming so close to the Kaka shambles, Chelsea, Man United and the whole of the media will be having a right good laugh at the expense of

Man City this weekend. Is it any wonder a few of their boys want to cover up their embarrassment with a few afters in the car park?

Sunderland Away

The recession is biting and for the first time in my career I find myself unemployed. It has been coming for months, but it is a situation that twelve months ago seemed unthinkable. Unlike many people who are being made compulsorily redundant on statutory minimum payouts, my situation is different. With my company reducing its workforce by twenty five thousand people worldwide and the relationship with our local client deteriorating beyond hope, it is an opportunity to exit on a good payout before I am kicked out with nothing. So on the one hand I cannot complain too much as I have enough financial cover to last twelve months before the panic alarms start sounding. On the other hand, signing on has been a new experience for me. Although Reading has a perceived affluence as a home-counties boomtown, things are pretty dire in the job market as the major telecoms and IT companies in the area are getting a hiding in the stock market. Money for football is not yet an issue, but clearly expensive away days and perhaps even next year's season ticket will become an unaffordable luxury if I do not find a new job soon.

Fortunately all the arrangements for Sunderland away were made before my final January pay packet, so I have no guilt about the expenditure for what is my longest away trip of the season. Reading to Sunderland, via London and Newcastle is just over seven hundred miles return. My brother and I got ourselves well organised and have picked up train tickets to The Stadium of Light for just over thirty quid return. With cheap match day tickets as well, it will probably end up being a cheaper day out than Chelsea away, a mere thirty miles down the road. It is my first full away day for a few months so I am eager to get to Kings Cross with plenty of time to spare to get breakfast and papers for the train. On arrival I find our 10:40am train cancelled and the next service means we will probably miss the kick off. I am told we can travel on the 10:30am service, but I cannot get hold of my brother and given his track record of arriving thirty seconds before the train departs, I am not confident he will be here in time.

I meet Mackem Chris in the concourse of Kings Cross while I am in the queue for the 10:30am train. Mackem Chris is a mate of my brother who now lives in Oxford and he is travelling to the game with us today. He was a tidy semi-professional player at his peak and is a keen Sunderland fan having been born in the North East. He is also in a bit of a panic about the cancelled train and cannot get hold of my brother either. He heads off to find some breakfast and the barrier for the 10:30am opens. There is a free for all for seats, but after barging a few students out of the way I manage to grab a table. The only question now is whether my brother will make it in time. I may have the dilemma of leaving my brother at Kings Cross if his usual time keeping is anything to go by. At 10:28am my phone goes and there is confirmation that Chris and my brother have hooked up and are on the train. They join me just as the train pulls out of Kings Cross. We can relax now and in a show of discipline we wait a whole half an hour before the first lagers are opened.

There are three other lads travelling up to Newcastle for the weekend on the next table and as they get through their lagers the banter and noise level in the carriage increases. It turns out they support Liverpool, Watford and Reading. Liverpool and Watford are definitely both armchair, but the Reading lad is a season ticket holder and so we are able to talk a bit about Reading. 'So how come you're not going today?' I ask.

'We're having a bit of weekend away in Newcastle', he says, looking a bit cagey.

'It seems a bit odd arranging it when Reading are playing

and pushing for promotion.'

'Well there's a bit of story, I'm serving a three month ban from The Madejski.'

This guy is no hooligan, so I am intrigued, 'Come on you've got to tell us what for.'

'Pitch encroachment.'

'Pitch encroachment? Which game?' I ask expecting him to refer to a last minute winner against one of the London or South Wales teams.

'Doncaster', he says looking a bit sheepish.

I am incredulous. 'You got yourself banned for celebrating the winner against Doncaster?'

'It was a bit beer induced and not my cleverest moment.'

On arrival in Newcastle we head straight for The Metro and arrive at The Stadium of Light about 2pm. On the approach to the ground we find a pub called The Colliery Arms. It is clearly a home supporter's pub, but with Sunderland having a reputation for friendliness and no Stoke colours on display we take a chance. A number of Potteries accents confirms it is fine and we get chatting to some Sunderland fans. They are confident of a home win now that their form has improved following the resignation of Roy Keane. A win for Sunderland will see them within a whisker of safety against relegation. That said, I think Sunderland were the poorest team we have seen at The Brit this season and following our win against Man City I am also confident we could see our first away win of the season today. We have a couple of pints and then Chris heads to the home end and my brother and I join up with the Stoke fans inside the stadium with plenty of time to spare.

The Stadium Of Light is without doubt one of the best stadiums in the country. Once inside, the atmosphere from both Stoke and Sunderland initially feels a bit muted. Perhaps there is a sense of dread about the quality of football we might be about to witness. My seat turns out to be on the end of the row and I am literally just a narrow gangway away from the home fans. With three thousand home fans in the corner next to us making all the home noise, it is hugely intimidating to be so close to them. There is abuse being hurled both ways across the line of stewards, but where I am it is all good-natured and there is no intervention from either police or stewards. The scene is set for a classic encounter.

It is a dreadful first half that sees Stoke unable to create any real chances despite going direct. Sunderland are just as bad as they are unable to break Stoke down. Both sides are limited to some half chances. I find myself utterly lost by Stoke's team selection, through a combination of having had a few too many and Stoke being forced to make three changes because of injuries. It takes most of halftime for my brother and I to work out what is going on. Stoke have signed Stephen Kelly and Henri Camara on loan. Kelly replaces Pugh in Higginbotham's position and Cresswell is again favoured in midfield over Lawrence, in what is a surprising and worrying decision by Pulis. A third change sees Amdy Faye replaced by Diao in midfield. Then Pugh replaces Wilkinson, Sonko replaces Shawcross and Camara replaces Fuller all before half an hour is played, with Fuller's injury looking particularly bad as he dislocates his shoulder.

There is just one first half incident of note and it is down to Rob Styles. It is a spectacularly bad decision even by his woeful standards. Pugh saves a goal bound header from Sunderland on the line with his arm. It simply has to be a penalty and a red card and I, along with two thousand other Stoke fans, cannot believe it when Styles gives a goal kick to Stoke. Sunderland's players and fans are incandescent while Stoke sing 'There's only one Rob Styles'. It is the only high point of a woeful forty five minutes.

Into the second half. The temperature plummets and the snow that cut off the South East earlier in the week has arrived on Wearside. It is bleak, but the football is even bleaker. It is turning into a 0-0 certainty that would look out of place in The Championship for its lack of quality, never mind The Premier League. Fortunately for the neutrals, Rob Styles is on hand to dish up some more controversy. Stoke are awarded a free kick, but in the same incident Etherington is given a straight red. Later, replays will show a little retaliatory kick by Etherington following the foul, but at the time nobody in the stadium has a clue. Now it is the Sunderland fans turn to taunt us. I shout over the steward at the Sunderland fan a couple of seats away, 'What was that for?' He shrugs, as clueless as me and gives me the 'going down' hand signal. Sunderland fancy this now against ten men.

Stoke still have the free kick. Whelan takes it. There is momentary chaos in the Sunderland box and the ball falls to an unmarked Camara just a couple of yards out. He must score, but instead slams a scoop shot against the bar, when it looks harder to miss than score. It is the defining moment as Sunderland take total control of the game for the last half an hour. Sunderland score with ten minutes left and seal the victory in injury time, much to the relief of the home fans. My brother and I both agree it is the worst performance of the season and the worst game of football we have seen for a long time. We head back to The Colliery Arms and meet Chris. He is happy with the result, but confirms the game was dreadful. The snow is coming down thick and settling quickly. There is a real grimness about Sunderland now and I really do not want to be stuck overnight.

By the time we get to The Metro it is a blizzard and there is a good couple of inches of snow on the ground. The Metro takes us back to Newcastle, but with only an hour to kill before our 7:30pm train to London we decide to stay on the station. There is a good bar showing the Portsmouth v Liverpool game. Liverpool must win to have any chance of winning the league, while Portsmouth now look in desperate relegation trouble. Liverpool do Stoke a big favour by winning 3-2 after trailing 2-1 with just five minutes left. Torres' injury time winner is the perfect kick in the teeth to Pompey just before they visit The Brit in our next game.

7:30pm and we make our way onto the platform for the

London train. There are three lads whose football shirts I do not initially recognise. The shirt sponsor is Dreams, which means they are supporting Wycombe Wanderers. We end up in the same carriage and after a bit of a sing off they join our card game and I am able to ask what they are doing on Newcastle station. It turns out Wycombe were due to play Darlington today, but the game was then postponed, so they went to the Sunderland v Stoke game instead. As if their day had not been bad enough, they managed to spoil it even more by shelling out thirty quid to watch a dire game. The cards and banter, particularly when Chris lets it slip that he used to play for Wycombe youth team, makes for a good journey back, but as I arrive back home after midnight I really am questioning the wisdom of following Stoke away this season.

Portsmouth Home

What feels like a rare 3pm Saturday afternoon kick off for a home game, sees the visit of FA Cup holders Portsmouth. Since the departure of Redknapp, Portsmouth's season has turned into a catastrophe following early Carling, FA and UEFA Cup exits coupled with a slump in Premier League form. Tony Adams has been sacked following Portsmouth's defeat by Liverpool and the immediate response saw them beating Man City. This change of management probably could not have been timed worse for Stoke as Portsmouth experience a bounce in form. This is Stoke's first of five consecutive home games against teams in the bottom eight. The next two months will tell us whether our own Man City win was the turning point in our relegation slide or nothing more than a blip as we plummet into the abyss. There is tension in the air as my dad, my brother and I take our seats in what is the first game all three of us have attended since the end of November.

Another big home crowd dwarfs the small following from Portsmouth. I had wondered if the crowds might start to tail off now that we have played all the glamour clubs at home. It is clearly not the case, as the home stands sold out days before the game. The positive news for Stoke is that the mini injury crisis appears to be over. Lawrence starts a game for the first time since the end of September and looks totally inspired to be playing. Pugh replaces the suspended Etherington and Sidibe returns from long-term injury to replace Fuller. There had been initial talk of Fuller being out for the rest of the season, but now it seems he might be available next week. Higginbotham returns to make up a full strength defence.

The first half is a stalemate with little incident of note. As the game wears on the initial noise in The Brit starts to wane. Portsmouth's defence look capable of dealing with everything thrown at them and despite their problems they look to have enough quality to catch Stoke on the counter. Halftime comes and goes and the game is heading for a drab 0-0 draw. The Brit is near silent for the first time this season as both sides snuff each other out. With fifteen minutes left, I feel that a draw will be OK today and I sense that both teams are thinking the same. It is not a game either side can afford to lose.

Such thoughts are premature as Stoke's defence is split open on seventy five minutes by a well-worked move between Nugent and Kranjcar. Kranjcar coolly place the ball under Sorenson and into the back the net. The halfhearted appeals for offside are futile and The Britannia stadium is silent except for the few hundred Portsmouth fans in the South Stand. This is bad and I head downstairs to empty my bladder. I am not alone downstairs and almost immediately there is a huge cheer from above. It is too short to be a goal, so I rush back upstairs just in time to see the referee surrounded by Portsmouth players and Beattie lining up a penalty kick. My brother suggests it was dodgy and even before Beattie's shot has hit the back of the net we are both receiving text messages suggesting it is a terrible decision by the referee. Finally the game has sprung into life.

We are still celebrating what feels like a lucky equaliser when Portsmouth are caught napping. A Wilkinson run stretches the Portsmouth defence and his deep cross finds Pugh. Pugh puts the ball back in and a Beattie header finishes the job. Two goals in ninety seconds means Stoke have to survive ten minutes for a priceless three points. Frankly it feels lucky. Just five minutes ago we were watching the worst home game of the season. Now it feels like a classic. More text messages suggest Beattie was miles offside. Is this the day that Stoke's luck changes? I don't know, but with three goals in four games it is definitely the day that Beattie enters potential legend status as Stoke's Premier League saviour.

Portsmouth look broken and their fans are silent. I am sure the game is won, but today I am really not sure how. Stoke close down the game and look comfortable. Portsmouth press, but are forced into speculative long shots. Deep into injury time and Hreidarsson takes a shot from right in front of us. I can see it is going miles wide and it must be the last kick of the game. I take my eye off the action for a split second because the shot is so tame. When I look back I see the ball deflecting past Sorenson and into the net in front of a stunned Boothen End. Shawcross is left with his head in his hands after slicing his clearance past Sorenson and into his own net. The Britannia Stadium is absolutely silent. Then the noise from the few remaining Portsmouth fans hits us, as they cannot believe they have got away with a draw. It is a desperately disappointing end to the game and one that ultimately could be so costly. On reflection though a draw was a more than fair result. Once I am home and watching Beattie's on-side goal on Match Of The Day I am left feeling pretty happy with the outcome, especially considering we have witnessed the worst penalty decision of the season go in our favour.

Villa Away

'We're staying up,' I say. My brother looks at me like I am totally deluded. 'Look, I've done the analysis,' and I hand him a printout of the spreadsheet I did after the Portsmouth game.

'You really have got too much time on your hands haven't you, you sad case?' he says. We are on the train from Reading to Birmingham. It is Sunday lunchtime and my brother is looking tired. For me the football is my only break from being in the house all week as the reality of being unemployed is starting to hit. I am disappointed my brother is not showing more enthusiasm for our day out at Villa Park. The one big positive about being at home all week is that I am feeling no guilt about weekend football anymore. I actually think Kate is glad to see the back of me on football days. How the situation has changed from a few weeks ago. Anyway being a 'sad case', I feel sure, having analysed the remaining twelve games for the bottom eight clubs, that Stoke will survive. The relegation battle is shaping up to be three from West Brom, Boro, Blackburn, Stoke, Spurs, Newcastle, Portsmouth and Hull.

Today we travel to Villa Park with no expectation whatsoever. Hopefully it will be a good day out with Stoke selling their entire allocation, but Villa are the team of the season having finally broken the monopoly of The Big Four. They looked destined for The Champions League and have even sacrificed the UEFA Cup this week to ensure they can put out their strongest team today against Stoke. We have got a couple of hours to kill before kick off when we arrive at Birmingham New Street. We head out of the station to try and find a pub showing football. There are a number of big Premier League games today because of the mid-week UEFA Cup football and with today being The League Cup final many of those games have been brought forward to lunchtime. It is not our intention, but we end up in a pub full of Blues fans watching Sheffield United v Birmingham City in a crunch Championship promotion game. I have met many other fans who have wished Stoke well this season, but I have a feeling it will not be the case in this pub. In fact Birmingham get beaten by a very controversial penalty and I feel sure that the Blues fans would like nothing better than to take out their frustrations on a couple of Clayheads. So it is head down, keep quiet and get a taxi to Villa Park.

Newcastle have lost again, but more interestingly Hull have lost at home to Blackburn. My brother lumped on Hull to be relegated at 9/2 earlier in the season, so we have been watching their slide down the table with glee. I feel sure Hull are going to be relegated after Phil Brown's David Brent impersonation on Boxing Day. The only downside is that Blackburn's win sees Stoke firmly back into the relegation zone before our game at Villa has even kicked off. The taxi drops us the wrong side of Villa Park and after a bit of hassle getting in, we are inside the ground right on 3:00pm. Spring has well and truly arrived and its t-shirt weather all round at a fabulous looking Villa Park. No surprise that the Stoke boys are up for it, but Villa are as well so once again the scene is set.

From almost the first minute I am struggling to understand Stoke's tactics. They basically appear to be playing a nine one zero formation. It is not helped that Abdoulaye Faye is replaced with Sonko at the back, but it definitely feels like Sidibe and Pugh are playing well out of position just in front of the full backs. With Amdy Faye and Diao playing their usual deep positions in midfield there is no outlet. Villa are invited to a party in Stoke's last third and on the rare occasion that a break looks on, the ball is just punted up field into no mans land. It is absolutely terrible. Villa cannot believe their luck, but they also look baffled as they try and break Stoke down. Sorenson makes a string of good saves, but right on halftime Petrov's strike makes it 1-0. For the first time this season, the 'boos' ring out from a large number of Stoke's travelling fans. I am not one for booing the team, but it really feels like enough is enough away from home. Match after match we have seen Stoke dead and buried after showing a total lack of adventure away from home. Given the time and money committed to following Stoke away this season we deserve better and today is the day that the frustration boils over.

There is no decent catering inside Villa Park so we are left to mull over what has gone wrong from the stands. The second half starts and Stoke revert back to an obvious four four two. They immediately look more organised. Ten minutes in and Fuller replaces Pugh. His impact is immediate as his pace troubles the Villa defence. Ten minutes later Whelan replaces Amdy Faye and Stoke now look genuinely dangerous for the first time. A Fuller turn and shot fizzes over the bar with Friedel beaten. Stoke are in the ascendancy and it is against the run of play when a Petrov cross finds Carew. Carew scores a cracking lob over Simonsen, who has replaced Sorenson at halftime. Villa Park erupts and with just ten minutes left the game is surely over.

A large number of Stoke fans head for the exits as the Villa fans taunt them. I suggest to my brother that we should also leave. I do not fancy queuing for Sunday trains with forty thousand others. He suggests we give it another five minutes. Villa now look complacent, even arrogant, but rather than whither and die Stoke are suddenly inspired to throw caution to the wind. A Shawcross header skims over the bar from a corner. Seconds later Whelan strikes a cracking shot that beats Freidal, but hits the post. Then its Fuller's turn to have a goal bound shot blocked out for a corner. Eighty eight minutes played and Beattie puts in a cross that Shawcross connects with and this time he hits the target with his header. It is his first Premier League goal, but there is no celebration on the pitch as Shawcross gathers the ball from the back of the net and returns it to the centre spot. The celebrations are muted in the stands also and there is a shout of 'Too little, too late Stoke'.

Three minutes of injury time are signalled as Stoke attack again. Villa are wobbling now. Fuller finds Sidibe, who shoots. The shot is blocked and time distorts as the ball falls in slow motion to Whelan on the edge of the box. His drilled shot is inch perfect and initially I am frozen as the ball hits the back of the net, in front of the open mouthed Brummies massed behind the goal. It is another one of those moments where the mind goes blank in a huge delirious celebration. It is the ultimate moment in a season of ultimate moments. It is a moment that should last a lifetime and yet I can remember virtually nothing. Minutes later I am breathless, shaking and so lightheaded I actually have to sit. The game finishes and the Stoke players celebrate in front of us. The Holt End boos off the Villa players and the Villa fans away to our right, who have been so vocal, have to suffer the ultimate humiliation of the Stoke taunts as they exit Villa Park.

Moments like this have been all too rare away from home this season and there is now a genuine air of optimism as we head for Whitton Park station. You do not need colours today to identify who supports who. Every Brummie looks glum, every Stokie looks ecstatic and there is enough banter in the streets of Aston to suggest things might turn ugly. At Whitton station the banter turns offensive, but the police are quick to nip it in the bud and a couple of Stoke lads are given a warning. I want to continue the singing, but now heavily out numbered by Villa fans and with the police taking a very active interest, it is time to calm down.

After the short train ride into Birmingham we still have an hour to kill so we head to a bar underneath The Midland Hotel. It is pretty quiet, but there are a couple of Villa fans in there. They do not look happy. On top of the recent FA Cup and UEFA Cup exits, their league form is taking a nosedive.

Villa's current league position is misleading as they look to rescue a season that is rapidly unravelling. The same could be said of Stoke's league position. Stoke are now nineteenth, but with five of the next six games looking winnable, there is every chance Stoke can still avoid the drop. I am left thinking Whelan's goal could be a major turning point, not only for Stoke, but also for Villa. My brother meanwhile looks like he is thinking it is time for bed.

Bolton Home

The dramatic finish at Villa Park, just over seventy two hours ago, got the TV pundits talking Stoke up. For the first time in months Stoke have made the headlines for all the right reasons. Tony Pulis has been getting some high profile recognition after admitting to getting it horribly wrong in the first half, but then having the tactical foresight to change it around at halftime. I have to admit to not being a huge fan of the tactics that, over recent seasons, have seen us grind out single goal wins. I also accept that just a couple of years ago I thought I would never see Stoke play in England's top division again. Not only that, but now it seems Stoke might have given themselves a great chance of staying there. The situation we fans find ourselves in is down solely to the professional relationship that exists between Tony Pulis and Peter Coates. I am no boo-boy, but I admit to being as fickle as the next man when it comes to football. All of us should take a step back and admire what has been achieved by Coates and Pulis in the last few years and particularly the professional way in which Tony Pulis has handled the media backlash against Stoke City this season.

Stoke still remain in the relegation zone and this is a serious fixture tonight that is unlikely to be one that appeals to the purists. I can almost imagine the BBC commentators drawing lots to avoid this bruising long ball encounter at a freezing Britannia Stadium. The fact that both Bolton and Stoke can occasionally play at bit will go unnoticed, but why worry about facts when there is a story to tell that needs to ensure the Premier League's unfashionable clubs remain as the league's villains.

Looking at the fixtures ahead, every game is starting to look like a six pointer. Bolton have been sitting just below mid-table for months, but cannot quite put a run together that will see them safely extract themselves from the relegation battle. Make no mistake Stoke v Bolton is a massive game and another home sell-out at The Britannia awaits. It is a night game so I have driven from Reading to Stoke and picked my dad up in Oxford. With time on my hands I had offered to drive into London to pick up my brother, but his work is hectic and he cannot get the time off. He will be following the game on the Internet in London.

Clearly the spring sunshine is yet to travel the forty miles up the M6 to thaw the Stoke-on-Trent permafrost. On Sunday I was wearing a t-shirt in Birmingham. Tonight the snow comes down again as a bone chilling wind whips through the open corners of The Britannia Stadium. This is going to be a proper blood and thunder English style match for the hardy. No Portuguese step-overs wanted here. Abdoulaye is back from injury and Delap is back from suspension as the battle of the Premier League bad boys gets underway.

The game lives up to the pre-match expectation as both teams battle it out at a frantic pace. Stoke make the early running and before fifteen minutes is reached, a poor kick from Jaaskelainen finds the head of Whelan who sends Beattie clear through. Beattie's class shows as he blasts the ball into the back of the net in front of The Boothen End. It is official. Beattie is now a Stoke City legend. Stoke control the game and from that point on it is comfortable. Although Bolton, and in particular Elmander, occasionally look dangerous, we are witnessing one of Stoke's best performances of the season and from the moment Beattie scores it never looks in doubt.

Fuller comes on as a substitute with half an hour left. As at Villa, there is no sign of injury and once again he looks fully committed to the cause. If Fuller has sorted himself out it will give Stoke great hope for the remainder of the season.

A Fuller/Beattie partnership could be the most dangerous in the bottom half of the table. As if to prove a point, Fuller fires home Stoke's second with fifteen minutes to go after Jaaskelainen can only parry a vicious shot from Whelan. Any nagging doubts that Stoke will not take all three points are erased. The game is won and won comfortably. At fulltime Stoke have recorded their first win by more than a single goal for thirteen months. Had Sonko's bullet header, near the end of the game, been two inches lower rather than crashing against the bar, it would have seen Stoke win a game by three goals for the first time since 2007.

Outside the ground I speak to my brother on the phone and he confirms my suspicion that tonight we are going to witness the most important night of the season so far for Stoke. Last night saw West Brom, Portsmouth and Sunderland lose. Tonight there is confirmation that Boro and Newcastle have both lost and Blackburn have been held at home. Hull are still drawing away at Fulham, but the late kick off means there are still fifteen minutes to play. Assuming Fulham find a winner, Stoke will rise five places to fourteenth in the table. The signing of James Beattie has changed our season and after a bleak mid-winter Tony Pulis is steering Stoke City towards Premier League survival.

Everton Away

Today is turning out to be an unashamed nostalgia trip for me. My brother is at a wedding so I have got an early train to Oxford and driven the one hundred and seventy miles up the M40, M6 and M62 with my dad. When I left Reading it was 2009, but now that I am standing in Goodison Park, half an hour before the kick off, I feel like I am back in the eighties. Part of this feeling is generated because most of Goodison Park has not changed for at least thirty years. Granted there are plastic seats on the old paddock terraces and the stand to our left which used to house the away fans has been re-developed, but the old stand where the away fans are now located, still has the Brazilian ghosts of 1966 wandering the concourse. Everything about the pre-match atmosphere, from the police horses in the terraced streets to the stick wielding sergeants outside the old decrepit turnstiles, makes this experience feel like it is from an age long forgotten.

However, I think the main reason for feeling like this today is because I am with my dad. Travelling to away games with him is becoming a rare event. I went to Coventry away with him last season, but this is our first away day this season. It is of course because of my dad that I am here at all. Thirty years ago it was my dad taking me to The Victoria Ground and when I was slightly older I remember him taking me to Kenilworth Road and Leeds Road to see Stoke play away. Over the years we have been to loads of away games, but more recently they have started to become few and far between and now it feels like the roles of who takes who have started to reverse. On the slow walk through Stanley Park I am a little nervous about how my dad may cope with the raucous away followings we have been experiencing this season. Even with our seats in row four, it is unlikely that he will see anything if he needs to sit. Once inside I realise this is unlikely to be a problem as my dad is well up for it. In the rammed concourse, I suggest we take our seats early, but he refuses, instead wanting to watch the end of Man United's humiliation to Liverpool being shown live on the screens.

The sense of nostalgia continues as the teams enter the pitch to the theme from Z Cars. The Stoke fans at the front of the bottom tier organise themselves with kids and OAPs taking the front row while everyone else remains standing. The suggestion that my dad does the same is shunned and it is clear he is up for the away day as much as anyone. I have a sudden pang of guilt that perhaps my brother and I should have made more effort to take him away this season, but in truth it was always going to be difficult to get him tickets when he is not on the priority list. Deliah rings out and I catch my dad joining in. He never normally does that. He thinks Deliah is a modern day fad amongst Stoke's supporters. The fact that Stoke's fans have been singing Deliah for over twenty years is apparently irrelevant. If it is not a song that predates the seventies then it is not a proper song.

Another inept first half performance by Stoke blows away the fluffy clouds of nostalgia. There is no real expectation of a result today, but once again Stoke have failed dismally on the road. It is the same team that so comprehensively beat Bolton and yet at halftime Stoke find themselves 2-0 down and there is little to suggest there will be a Villa or Newcastle style recovery. Everton's goals came close together, from Jo and Lescott, and for once Sorenson looked at fault for the first. The big screen replay shows Lescott well offside, but in truth there can be little complaint about the score at halftime.

The second half starts and the majority of Stoke's fans are more intent on trying to get a reaction from the silent Everton fans than watching a game that is lost. All the Scouse classics come out and when a Vicky Pollard look-a-like is spotted on the home end there is a moment of comic genius as three and half thousand Stoke fans direct the singing her way. She is utterly oblivious. In the end her mate draws her attention to it and she takes it all in good spirits by giving the Stoke boys the two-fingered salute.

On the pitch I am almost oblivious to the fact that Stoke have at last deployed some adventurous tactics. Everton look complacent and Stoke must have had a rocket from Pulis at halftime. Stoke win a corner that is delivered by Lawrence right onto the head on an unmarked Shawcross. His glancing header surprisingly beats Tim Howard and finds the bottom corner. Now it is game on. Fuller replaces Sidibe with half an hour left Stoke go forward in search on an equaliser. Fuller causes problems and just minutes later Stoke win another corner. Lawrence delivers and Higginbotham connects a header, that flies just wide of the post, as Shawcross comes within millimetres of making a vital connection that would see the ball in the back of the net. When a Whelan shot fizzes inches wide of the top corner, I start to fear that Stoke may have missed their chance today. That fear is confirmed in injury time when Everton score their third on the break as Stoke continue to press. 3-1 flatters Everton, as they become only the third team to do the double over Stoke this season.

I walk back through Stanley Park with my dad and we both agree it has been a good day today. It has been worth the trip and Stoke can count themselves unlucky after the second half performance. A number of results go against Stoke and rather harshly they drop back into the relegation zone. However with the next four games against teams in the bottom six and three of those four games at home, Stoke's Premier League destiny is still very much in their own hands.

Middlesbrough Home

The most important few weeks of the season approach. Despite remaining in the relegation zone, Stoke have given themselves every chance of Premier League survival and hope remains very much alive. The build up to the Boro game is huge with Pulis and Southgate making regular television interviews. I have been genuinely nervous for days before the game. During the week I was in touch with my old housemate Dan. He is Boro through and through. We both agreed that whichever team loses today will probably get relegated. We are set for another vital six pointer.

Yesterday I received a formal job offer and I will start back at work on April 14th. It means I will have spent just ten weeks unemployed. In the current economic climate I am a very lucky man. My first expenditure is the renewal of my season ticket. Kate has made no pretence that she is going to clip my wings significantly next season, but even if I miss a few home games, the season ticket is such good value I would be stupid not to take up the offer. I will choose my moment carefully for when I break the news to her about my purchase.

This morning I got the train over to Oxford and met my dad and brother. I arrived at Oxford station early and decided to get the local bus out to Oxford Park and Ride. I found my dad and brother tucking into the sandwiches and sausage rolls that my mum provides for us at every home game. This season my mum has undergone a football transformation. My dad is forever telling us the story of West Ham away when he was dating my mum in London during the sixties. Stoke were 3-0 down at Upton Park and came back to win 4-3. Apparently my mum was 'bored to tears' by the whole experience. This season, for the first time she has got drawn into the football and has watched Stoke's games live on Sky, got to know most of the player's names and is glued in front of Soccer Saturday. It is a transformation as unexpected as the one that we have witnessed with the club itself.

Given where both teams are in the table, there is no expectation that this game will be a classic and both Boro and Stoke deliver to meet our expectations. It is a terrible game that has 0-0 written all over it. Boro defend well and look organised up until the last third, but up front they are totally impotent. I would suggest this is the sentence that describes Boro's entire season. When Boro beat Stoke back in August it was their best ever start to The Premier League. Since then they have experienced a calamitous slide down the table, taking some absolute thrashings on the way. They look certain for the drop and nothing I witness today would suggest otherwise. A large and noisy following from Boro makes for an intense atmosphere inside The Brit and for eighty five minutes the Boro fans get behind their team. They know they are in the doorway of last chance saloon and do everything to will their team to survival. It is the best away following witnessed at Stoke this season.

There is genuinely only one incident of note in the entire game. It really is that tight. With five minutes left Stoke do not look like scoring, but neither do Boro so as full time approaches it looks like the points will be shared. Stoke get a throw deep into the Boro half and Delap fires it in. Boro have dealt easily with everything thrown at them today by Delap, but in a split second there is a lack of concentration and Shawcross is left unmarked. He connects the header and it so simple it almost looks like a training ground goal. The reaction around the stadium is an indication of just how important the goal is. How ironic that moments earlier Boro's fans were suggesting we were only there for the throw ins. It is the first Delap long throw inspired goal for months and it kicks the wind out of

Boro and their fans. Stoke cruise to the three points and the Boro fans turn on their players and manager. Boro are going down and after the game hundreds of Stoke fans gather on the embankments behind The South Stand. This is to ensure, as they board their coaches, the Boro fans know it is now a hopeless cause.

West Brom Away

About six weeks ago I came downstairs to find Kate opening a very fancy looking letter and I instantly knew it was a wedding invitation. My immediate thought was, which Saturday is now at risk from somebody selfishly getting married in the middle of the football season? Weddings in the football season should be banned. 'We've been invited to my cousin's wedding,' says Kate opening the letter.

'Oh that's great', I reply trying to sound enthusiastic. Oh no, not just a wedding, but a family wedding.

'In Valencia,' Kate continues, now audibly excited.

'Fantastic! When is it?'

'April 4th'. West Brom away, the most important away game of the season and unless I do something to prevent it, I will be in Spain with Kate's family during what could be Stoke's defining moment of the season.

'Are we all invited?'

'Just you and me.'

'So what about the kids?'

'Can't we leave them with your parents.'

'I don't know, they're not getting any younger and we'll probably have to be away for four or five nights. It doesn't seem right to leave them especially if your parents are away as well. I tell you what why don't you go and I will stay and look after the kids.' I am thinking on my feet here.

Kate looks suspicious at my charitable offer. 'OK, we'll see.'

I phone my mum while Kate is in the shower. 'Hi mum'.

'Oh, hi Steve, how are you?'

'Good thanks, listen mum, are you doing anything on April 4th?'

There is a long pause while she gets the calendar. 'No, looks OK, why what's up?'

'Any chance you can have the kids on Saturday afternoon?' Am I really this devious?

So that is how it happened and boy did I pay the price. On Thursday I took Kate up to the M40 so that her sister and Jon could pick her up and take her down to Gatwick. Jon is not too impressed that I managed to exit out of the wedding. I get home, pick the kids up from school and by 7:30pm they are in bed. I settle down with a glass of wine and contemplate five nights of being a single father. No matter how bad this turns out I have the West Brom game to look forward to. At 8:30pm my youngest wakes up crying and when I go upstairs she is burning up.

Two days later and I take my seat on the 12:10pm train from Oxford to Birmingham. I have not slept properly for forty eight hours. My youngest timed her illness to perfection and was awake all Thursday night, off school on Friday and awake again all of Friday night. Kate is obviously concerned when she calls, but I can tell she is thinking that this is finally payback time for all the times she has nursed the kids, while I have slept through. Fortunately this morning my daughter was much better, so I drove over to Oxford and left both the girls with my mum and dad for the afternoon. What a joy it is to chill out on the train with a paper and have time to put thought into today's game. My brother is on the train from London and we will meet in Birmingham. At Banbury station I read a fact in the paper that is spookily coincidental. Banbury Town and Stoke City are the only two teams in the top four hundred or so professional and semi-professional teams not to have won away from home this season. Today we play West Brom, so given our record against them, I think that is about to change.

I arrive in Birmingham at 1:30pm and head to the bar on

the station to wait for my brother. He meets me about half an hour later. There is a train to Smethwick Rolfe Street about to depart, but we decide to wait for the next one and have a pint instead. I know Birmingham well, having lived there for three years and I have been to The Hawthorns many times. However, I have never been there by train via Smethwick Rolfe Street. For some reason I have got it into my head that the station is right by the ground. We just make the 2:40pm departure, but there is not a single football fan on board. I start to panic that I have made a catastrophic error on the transport today. The train journey takes less than ten minutes, but on arrival there is not any suggestion that a football match is taking place today and there is no sign of The Hawthorns. My brother, rightly so, is less than impressed by my organisation. 'West Brom', I grab the nearest passer by, 'are we near West Brom?'

'What?'

'The Hawthorns, where is it, which direction?' My brother is on the phone looking seriously unhappy.

'It's about two miles that way,' the stranger points. Oh my god, what a disaster.

'I'm so sorry, I've totally cocked up.' I tell my brother.

'Chill, I've just called a cab. It'll be here in a couple of minutes.'

We arrive at The Hawthorns dead on 3pm and the cabbie takes us right to the turnstiles. Just as we are entering the ground there is a huge cheer, but it is not huge enough to suggest it is the home support. I think Stoke have scored. The steward on the gate confirms with his mate that West Brom are losing. Stoke have scored in the first two minutes of the game. We desperately run up to the stand to join the celebrations. By now I have lost my brother and am celebrating with some random as I get confirmation that Fuller has scored.

Once things calm down I find our seats and find my brother. Nobody is sitting so we squeeze into our row near our seats. It is a full strength, first choice Stoke team and for the first time this season Stoke are utterly dominant away from home. Last week Stoke gave Boro a good hard shove through the door into last chance saloon. Inside Boro would have found West Brom slumped over the bar. West Brom appear doomed to relegation and defeat today, at home to Stoke, will be the nail in the coffin. The Stoke fans are rampant. The rest of The Hawthorns is totally silent as they ponder a Boxing Day visit to Doncaster next season.

It remains 1-0 to Stoke at halftime. Stoke have conceded possession, but have won the midfield battle and looked dangerous on the break. My brother and I head downstairs full of confidence that today will be the day for Stoke's first away win. Another goal will surely seal it. There is a big queue at the burger bar and by the time we get upstairs the game has kicked off again. Burger in hand, I head to our seats. Etherington breaks down the line and is tackled. I can't really see what happens, but the ball is fired into the back of the net and the celebrations are wild. I try and get on a seat, but get knocked over onto the floor in the celebrations. Hands pull me back up onto my feet and the celebrations continue. There is still most of the second half to play, but West Brom are so bad victory feels assured.

As things calm down, I get a pat on the back from the guy behind who had hauled me up. 'Best save of the day youth.' He nods at my intact burger in my hand. My brother's hot dog has been destroyed in the melee. Beattie is confirmed as the goal scorer and now it is serious party time at The Hawthorns. Stoke cruise to their first away win in the top-flight for twenty five years. May 1984 was when Stoke won away at Kenilworth Road in the old Football League Division 1. I am sure there were plenty more incidents in the game, but I can remember none of them. All I remember is the incessant taunting of The Baggies fans for the entire duration of the second half. West Brom have spent four seasons out of the last seven in The Premier League but have been relegated three times. Even though it is very harsh for them to take, there is no sympathy from where I'm standing. When the final whistle blows, the victory is huge. Not one Stoke fan has left and all the team come to the away end to celebrate on the pitch. With thirty five points on the board, safety is now tantalisingly close as Stoke move above Hull, Portsmouth and Sunderland, to thirteenth in the table.

Newcastle Home

It appears football pundits are even more fickle than football fans. Following Stoke's win against West Brom there is now real belief everywhere that Stoke will not be relegated. The pundits and journalists who laughed at Stoke last summer are now suddenly trying to jump on the Stoke City bandwagon. Everywhere in the press and on TV the football experts are trying to save face by praising Stoke and their fans. Never has a club newly promoted to The Premier League had the media hostility experienced by Stoke. It is something that will not easily be forgiven. Stoke have taken twenty three years to get back to the top division and there is no desire to return to The Football League just yet.

There are some people though who continue to ridicule Stoke City. There is still suggestion that Stoke deserve to be relegated because they are a small club, because their fans are hooligans or because they are a dirty negative side. Whilst early in the season such suggestion was widespread, the talk now appears to be coming solely from just one place in England. That place is Newcastle. Stoke have proven that success can come when a club is well organised, is financially sound and the fans get behind the team. Stoke City is everything Newcastle United is not. Stoke are one win from safety, Newcastle find themselves in the relegation zone.

Newcastle are onto their fourth manager this season and have now put their faith in a football pundit with no management experience to try and save them from the drop into The Championship. Clubs like Stoke, Boro and West Brom will survive financially if they get relegated. Newcastle meanwhile, with fifteen players on over fifty thousand pounds per week and no relegation clause in their contracts, are likely to end up like Leeds United if they fall off The Premier League gravy train. The whole media circus that surrounds Newcastle United has built up today's clash at The Britannia Stadium as one of the biggest games of the season. In truth Stoke can even afford to drop points.

The game is a late kick off because of live coverage on Setanta. My dad is at home, as my mum is unwell. I have driven up to The Britannia on my own and picked up my brother from Stoke station. He got the train up from Bristol today. When I meet him I realise I will be driving all the way back as well. Earlier today Boro beat Hull. Hull are now firmly in the relegation battle and the result also means Newcastle drop to nineteenth in the table before the game kicks off. It makes this evening's game a must win for them. Truth be told, it seems unfathomable that Newcastle are in the position they are in, given the resources they have. Once the game kicks off it is clear why Newcastle really could be going down this year. They are absolutely dreadful. They have Owen and Ameobi up front. Owen looks way past his best and every Stoke fan already knows how bad Ameobi is. He actually got dropped from Stoke's side in The Championship, when he was on loan last season.

Stoke control the game and it feels, from very early on, that Stoke will get a comfortable win this evening. There is passion on all sides of the stadium, but the Newcastle fans soon become quiet once it is becomes obvious they are in for a very tough encounter. Half an hour played and Stoke get a corner. Lawrence plays it in and Abdoulaye Faye connects an easy header. 1-0 and for the second time this season he celebrates a goal in front of the club that released him. Abdoulaye Faye is fast becoming a Stoke City cult hero and is clearly going to be named player of the season. Newcastle released him for a pittance by Premier League standards. Can there be any clearer indictment of Newcastle's turmoil than the sale of Abdoulaye

Faye to Stoke back in the summer?

Halftime comes and goes and Stoke need the second killer goal. Newcastle have not had a single chance all game so 1-0 might be sufficient. Stoke are all over Newcastle with Fuller causing them real problems. Fuller has undergone a transformation since dislocating his shoulder. All the petulance is gone and he has stepped up and scored a couple of vital goals in recent weeks. He now looks every bit a top drawer Premier League player and alongside Beattie it makes for a formidable partnership. Good chances fall to Whelan and Fuller. The Delap long throw is not being dealt with and Abdoulaye Faye has a header cleared off the line. With twenty minutes to play I cannot believe it is still only 1-0. It has been the most one-sided game I have seen at The Britannia Stadium all season. Cresswell replaces Beattie and Carroll replaces Ameobi. Stoke shut up shop in an attempt to hold the 1-0 lead. There is nothing to suggest it won't be a straightforward task.

Ten minutes left and Newcastle get a throw. It is taken long and Stoke fail to deal with it. The resulting cross finds Carroll and he brilliantly heads the ball past Sorenson. It is Newcastle's first attempt on goal. It is totally against the run of play and the Toon Army celebrate like they have won the league. It is a massive goal that ultimately secures a vital point for Newcastle as the game fizzles out into a draw. Stoke are happy with a point today, but really should have had more. Newcastle will go home happier, but a point does not really help their cause. They have winnable home games left, which will probably mean they will stay up, but it really is a sign of how bad things are at Newcastle when they celebrate getting a point at Stoke to the extent that they did.

Blackburn Home

The Saturday after Easter sees another sell out at The Brit for Stoke's second home game in a row against relegation rivals. A win today will surely see Stoke safe. Blackburn have had a very poor season by their standards, but Sam Allardyce looks to have done enough to steer them towards Premier League safety. A draw is the likely result today as both teams will be fearful of losing. I have little expectation of an open, flowing game as I take my seat with my dad. My brother is at a wedding today so I travelled up to Stoke with just my dad.

Stoke start with their strongest team for the third game in a row. They almost get off to a flying start, when a Whelan volley is nearly turned in by Beattie, after Delap's first long throw is not cleared. A minute later Fuller breaks clear and his cross just beats the outstretched foot of Etherington. Stoke look well up for it whilst Blackburn look shell-shocked. The game settles as Blackburn organise themselves. After the initial excitement the game turns into the dour stalemate we expected. Stoke have a couple of optimistic shouts for a penalty, but halftime is reached without major incident as both teams grind each other down.

It is more of the same after halftime, but Stoke are on top as they attack The Boothen End. Blackburn look very poor today. Whelan shoots wide and Lawrence has a shot tipped over the bar, but Stoke do not create many chances. It is definitely not a bad Stoke performance but, with both teams cancelling each other out, it is turning out to be one of the worst games seen at The Brit this season. The Boothen End cranks up the noise and the rest of The Britannia Stadium follows the lead.

Blackburn have sold their allocation today and have brought a vocal support down the M6, but it is no match for Stoke's support as they try and lift the team.

Fifteen minutes left and a Beattie flick finds Lawrence on the edge of the box. The defence is split and Lawrence just has the full back to beat. He dummies to go wide, but cuts back inside leaving the Blackburn defender flat-footed. It creates just enough space for Lawrence to release a vicious shot. Robinson gets a good hand to it, but the power takes the ball past him and it bobbles in the six yard box towards the goal. The Boothen End sucks the ball into the net. The celebrations are wild in the stands and on the pitch. It is the goal that ensures Premier League safety. Lawrence was so key to Stoke being promoted last year. For him to miss so much of the season through injury and then struggle to regain his place in the team must have been so difficult to deal with. In the last few games he has been outstanding and this is his Premier League moment. How apt that it is Lawrence that scores the goal that ensures Stoke stay in Premier League for another season.

Blackburn pressure Stoke in the final few minutes, but it is never really in doubt. The final whistle sparks delirious celebrations on and off the pitch. The return of binary football has taken some of the emotion out of the games in recent months, but as I make my way to the exit I am unexpectedly caught with a tear in my eye and a lump in my throat. As I look across the stadium, the joy expressed on The Boothen End is so raw you cannot help but be overcome by it. Stoke-on-Trent and Stoke City have seen some tough times. Tough times breed tough men. To see genuine hard men so wrapped up in the emotion of the moment is something I will never forget. That moment cannot be described. You simply had to have been there to know what it meant.

Fulham Away

It is a glorious sunny day and I am looking out over The River Thames. I am with my brother and we are basking in the glory of Premier League survival. It is so nice and relaxed that it feels a shame to spoil it by heading inside the ground to watch another poor performance away from home. So we don't. Instead we order another beer from Lager Man. As he passes us a couple of bottles from his back pack we settle down to watch the start of the second half on a plasma screen behind the stand. Hundreds of Stoke fans are doing the same. In many ways it is utterly ridiculous to spend thirty five quid on a ticket and then watch the game behind the stand on the TV. Today though, with the beautiful weather, a River Thames backdrop and another poor second half beckoning it is the right decision. Can there be any better location in The Premier League than Craven Cottage to revel in the achievement of survival? I don't think so. Without Higginbotham, Wilkinson and Beattie, Pugh, Kelly and Cresswell started the game today and Stoke have looked poor in the first half. I don't think it is a case of complacency. Rather Fulham are well organised and look good value for their eighth position in the table. Fulham are 1-0 ahead after a slick counter attack on the half hour.

A run of eighteen points from ten games has all but guaranteed Premier League survival for Stoke. There are still five games left, so it is not a mathematical certainty yet, but with Stoke placed eleventh in the table there is more chance of them finishing in a European place than in the bottom three. How things have changed over the last two and a half months. So what is the target now? Seventh place would see Stoke in

Europe. That is an unlikely target and if we are honest a place in the inaugural Europa League would be a poison chalice for Stoke. A top half finish though would be exceptional and would see Stoke's best league placing for thirty three years. Fulham have also had an exceptional season and have very realistic European ambitions. This follows an astonishing turnaround from last season, when they survived on goal difference with just minutes to spare.

Today should have been my shortest trip of the season to see Stoke, but instead I started off this morning from Gosport. Another wedding is on the horizon and this is one I do not want to miss. One of my oldest schoolmates is getting married in two weeks and this weekend is the stag do. Last night I was out in Portsmouth celebrating with the boys. My mates are off to The Isle of Wight on a chartered yacht today, but I bailed out of the trip, partly because of Stoke's game at Fulham, but mainly because it is my youngest daughter's birthday party tomorrow.

I ended up getting the Gosport Ferry this morning at 9:30am after sleeping rough on the deck of the yacht. I met my brother at his flat in Hammersmith at midday after the train journey up from Portsmouth. We started off in his local by Hammersmith Bridge where we met his mate Welsh Jonny. Not surprisingly Welsh Jonny is an egg chaser so he was not coming to the game. He was just there for some lunchtime beers. We made the short walk to The Crabtree Tavern. My brother knows this area of London well and it turned out to be the perfect pre-match pub with a large and friendly contingent of Fulham fans and plenty of Stokies enjoying themselves in the sun. We met one of my brother's mates who is a season ticket holder at Fulham. Bizarrely he is from Brisbane and has a daft Australian name like Bonza or something.

Bonza (and let us assume that is his name) turned out to be a top bloke. He has been in the UK for less than a year and is really a rugby league fan. However he has become completely obsessed with soccerball since arriving in the UK.

Being a season ticket holder at Fulham, there is no doubt that he is well into his footy, but there is something to suggest he does not always get it. For instance, he has been known to say things like, 'Did you know that Exeter have conceded the least number of goals of any team that have ever been promoted from The Conference?' and then immediately (with complete sincerity) follow it up with something along the lines of, 'The FA Cup, is that a knock out competition?' Spending a couple of hours with Bonza, Welsh Jonny and my brother led to the most random pre-match build up of the season.

My brother and I finish our beers and head back to our seats with about thirty five minutes left to play. The Stoke boys are in full voice and Pantsil is getting loads of stick. The Fulham fans are silent. To be fair to Stoke they make a much better game of it in the second half. Fuller causes plenty of problems and Stoke have a number of good half chances from set pieces. It ends up being one of those games where it just doesn't happen. The match statistics will show Stoke had just two shots on target and that says it all really. The result sees the European dream, albeit a remote one, quashed for a second time this season.

We meet Bonza outside the main stand and head back to The Crabtree. Then we hook up with Welsh Jonny in the pub garden and shortly afterwards Bonza's girlfriend and her mate join us. There are a few Stokies in the pub and then my brother clocks Smudge walking across the car park after the game. With Smudge being The Oatcake legend that he is, I suddenly feel like we are in the presence of a celebrity. It is a bit uncalled for, but I shout 'Alright Smudge?' across the car park. I do not know Smudge, so he would have every right to say 'Alright lads?' and carry on his way. However Smudge comes over and we have a long chat about the game and the season. He is a top man and being in the presence of such a legend makes for a great end to the day.

West Ham Home

Mid-table mediocrity is now the destiny that awaits Stoke City this season. These are words that last summer we could only have dreamed of. It now looks likely Stoke will finish between eleventh and fourteenth in the table. A mid-table finish is a fabulous achievement and of course it has been anything but mediocre. West Ham are still very much in the race for seventh, along with Man City, Fulham and Spurs so they have everything to play for in today's game at The Britannia Stadium. Like Hodgson at Fulham, Zola has excelled at West Ham since taking over as manager. He has steered West Ham from the brink of relegation to the brink of Europe. There is a risk that Stoke might now tail off this season, but with an additional seven hundred and fifty thousand pounds for every place higher up the league that Stoke finish, it is important to remain focussed until the end. A win today will ensure mathematical safety, but it is looking increasingly likely that thirty nine points will be comfortably enough to avoid relegation this season. The relegation battle is shaping up to be one of Hull, Newcastle or Sunderland to join Boro and West Brom.

The 3pm Saturday kick off means I follow my standard Saturday match day routine. Both my dad and brother meet me in Oxford at lunchtime. The Brit is sold out again with West Ham filling their allocation. The West Ham boys are in vocal mood as the game kicks off. Beattie and Wilkinson both return and Stoke start strongly. It takes just ten minutes for Fuller to find the back of the net as he bundles in a Delap long throw. The referee disallows it for a foul on the keeper.

No complaints at the time, but replays suggest Fuller is hard done by. At the other end West Ham put the ball in the net within sixty seconds of Fuller's goal being disallowed, but this is also ruled out for handball. It looks a harsh decision. The score should probably be 1-1.

Scuffles in The South Stand begin to distract my attention as once again the game starts to fall into a familiar stagnant pattern. Few chances are created, as the trouble in The South Stand starts to get out of hand. A large number of West Ham fans are clearly fighting with the Stoke stewards as they try and breach the no man's land. The Stoke fans are goading them on the other side of the plastic sheeting. West Ham get a free kick in a dangerous position as the police move in to sort out the fighting. It is the first major trouble inside The Britannia Stadium that I've seen for a very long time. Tristan blasts the free kick into the top corner past Sorenson. West Ham's fans go mental as they look to become the first team in 2009 to take three points home from Stoke-on-Trent. The score remains 1-0 to West Ham at halftime as the trouble is brought under control. There will be a few Cockneys taking the early train today.

West Ham look effective in holding a dominant Stoke in the second half, as The Boothen End will The Potters to get an equaliser. Good chances fall to Fuller and Lawrence. Abdoulaye Faye connects on a Delap long throw and the ball is cleared off the line. It feels like Stoke must score as the corners and long throws rain in. West Ham waste time as they close in on a huge three points. Ninety minutes is reached and it looks like West Ham will join Everton, Man United and Chelsea as the only teams that will do the double over Stoke this season. Two minutes into injury time and the ball falls to Fuller on the edge of the six yard box. He turns and shoots. The opportunity is gilt edged, but the ball is skyed over the bar. It is not going to happen for Stoke today despite a strong second half performance. At the end of the game there are huge celebrations from West Ham's fans and players. It shows what a big result it is for them, but is also another sign of the huge respect Stoke are now demanding at The Britannia Stadium.

Hull Away

Back in October I looked ahead at Stoke's fixture on May 9th and thought that will be the day that Stoke get relegated. It will be destiny for the whipping boys of 2008/9 to be relegated by the new darlings of The Premier League. I had the fear that I would board the train to Hull knowing we would have to suffer that ultimate humiliation. Phil Brown would be there, smiling smugly, while Hull City's fans sing 'You're getting mauled by the tigers'. The Stoke fans would brave it out of course, but it would go down as one of the most miserable days (and there have been many) in Stoke City history. We would return home on the train knowing a return to The Championship is assured and mid-table mediocrity of the very mediocre kind will be the best we can look forward to next season.

What a difference five months makes. Today is not just one of the biggest games of the season, it is the biggest game in Hull City's history. Hull's cataclysmic fall from grace has been the most spectacular ever witnessed in the top flight. Hull have to play Bolton away and Man United at home in their last two games. Form suggests zero points from those two games. Defeat to Stoke today will almost certainly see Hull relegated, assuming Newcastle beat Boro on Monday night. It is not a scenario I could have envisaged even in my wildest dreams. Another scenario I could not have envisaged was sitting in a church service in Portsmouth as the game is about to kick off.

This morning, as I was driving down the M27, my brother sent me a picture of a can of Carlsberg next to our Hull away tickets as his train departed Kings Cross. The caption was

'Enjoy the Wedding!' All week I have been wondering how it would have been if Stoke had needed something from this game. Would I have missed the wedding of one of my oldest mates to go and watch Stoke play instead? I am genuinely not sure, but since I made the decision to give up my ticket it has felt like the right thing to do. I complained bitterly to my mate about organising his wedding in the football season. He pointed out that it is only the football season for glory hunting Premier League fans and that the season has already finished for proper Football League fans. He supports Oxford United and his wife-to-be supports Brighton. Fair point, well made, but what about the playoffs I suggested? The look I got confirmed that playoff football had not been a consideration for either Oxford or Brighton for quite some time.

I am sitting behind an old school mate, Bugs, in the church. He supports Leeds and their game against Millwall has just kicked off in the League 1 playoff semi-final. As a fellow football fan suffering wedding syndrome I should have sympathy, but he supports Leeds and let's be honest, nobody likes Leeds, even if they are playing Millwall. Bugs has not got a phone where he can get the scores, so ten minutes into the wedding service, with the score 0-0, I lean over the pew and whisper, 'Bugs, 1-0 to Leeds.'

'Get in, come on you Mighty Whites.'

'Ahhh, not really.' The wind up is not appreciated and we get a 'Sssh' from the Wags.

I wait ten minutes and lean over the pew again. 'Bugs, seriously mate it really is 1-0 now.' He ignores me. Kate takes my phone and tells me to behave. I try again. 'Bugs, honest mate, I wouldn't wind you up twice.'

He doesn't turn round, but whispers, 'You're a dead man if you're winding me up again.'

'Honest.'

'Yes' and he clenches his fist.

'Ahhh, not really.' I could probably do this for the rest of the service, but I leave it there.

After the service I avoid Bugs. He is hard and is unlikely to appreciate the humour now that Leeds are losing 1-0. I congratulate Nim and Cathy outside the church. Then we head to Southsea in the car for the reception. It is now 3pm and Radio 5 goes on despite the protests from my two daughters. Hull versus Stoke is the feature game, so for once I stamp my authority on the in-car entertainment. Deliah rings out. It is pretty much impossible to follow the game on the radio whilst driving around Portsmouth. All I get is a sense that Stoke are in control, but the referee has ruled a couple of marginal decisions in favour of Hull. We arrive at our hotel and check in.

After dropping our gear in our room, I head down to the bar. As I walk past the hotel's reception I can see Soccer Saturday on the screen ahead and at the bottom it says 'Hull 0–1 Stoke - Fuller 41.' I shout 'Yes' and do a little skip with a clenched fist. The receptionist jumps, looking startled. There is no one else in the bar. I apologise, but she is less than amused. Halftime arrives and Fuller is shown leaving the field at The KC Stadium. I have no idea about the team or the performance, but I don't really care with the score being 1-0. We head over to the wedding reception and I try to call my brother. Initially the phones are jammed, but when I get through there is too much background noise and we cannot hear each other.

There is little opportunity to follow the second half once I am at the wedding reception. 5pm arrives, I make my excuses and leave the table to find a quiet corner at the back of the pub. My phone takes an age to connect, but eventually the score is confirmed as Hull 1-2 Stoke. It is a surreal moment. Here I am, alone in a quiet corner of a Southsea pub and in the instant it takes for my phone to display the final score I realise that three hundred miles away I am missing the ultimate climax to the ultimate season for Stoke City. Stoke are mathematically safe and Hull look certain to be relegated. I skim the match report and the win appears to be deserved with Lawrence scoring Stoke's winner.

Three hours later I finally get to speak to my brother. His train has just arrived back at Kings Cross. I get the full match report and whilst of course I am able to share in the delight of what has been achieved, I feel sick at missing out on one of Stoke's best ever away days. I can accept missing another vociferous Stoke away following. There will be other big away games next season. I can accept missing a stunning winner from Lawrence. Although rare I have no doubt there will be other stunning Stoke goals. I can accept missing the tension of the dying moments of the game (Hull score five minutes into injury time and then clip the outside of the post with a deflected shot), which almost sees Hull find the equaliser that would probably keep them in the Premier League. There will be more injury time drama next season. What I cannot stomach though, is missing the priceless moment of 'He's taking you down, he's taking you down, your Oompa Loompa, he's taking you down!'

Wigan Home

My brother is driving the car up the M40 for the last time this season. My dad is in the back. We are three fat Stoke fans in a Toyota Yaris. My brother is often quiet on these journeys, but today he is full of the trip away to Hull. I am genuinely interested, but I cannot help feeling I have put in more miles than him this season and yet I am the one who has missed two of the biggest moments. The equaliser at Newcastle and the win at Hull will surely go down in Stoke City folklore in years to come. Between us we will have been to all but two of Stoke's thirty eight Premier League games. After next weekend I will have been to thirty four and he will have been to twenty seven Stoke games this season. Given the transport logistics and expense involved, it is not a bad effort.

Arriving at The Brit for the last time for three months feels a bit odd. After all the tension that has gone before, this game with Wigan feels like a bit of an anti-climax. There is a real end of season feel to it, with both teams now having little to play for. It is a world away from the tense end of season encounter this time last year that saw Leicester relegated and Stoke promoted. Even so, the home stands are sold out again today and if it were not for the pitiful following from Wigan it would be another complete sell out. It seems that the Wigan players went on holiday weeks ago after securing Premier League safety. Wigan were right up there challenging for Europe, but a run of one point from their last six games now sees them just one place above Stoke on goal difference. Before our game kicks off we watch Man United win the Premier League again on the TV in the concourse after they draw 0-0 with Arsenal in the early match.

A party atmosphere today more than compensates for any lack of tension. There is plenty of fancy dress on show and inflatables a plenty in the stands. Despite now entering late Spring, the Stoke-on-Trent weather is going to deliver us one final blustery afternoon. It is the same Stoke team that started at Hull, so Cort retains his place and Pugh is on the bench. Other than that it is a full strength starting line up. The first half is dreadful. Wigan are definitely on the beach and it seems Stoke may have similar thoughts. The only highlight sees Delap throw the ball straight into the net without anyone getting a touch. It had to happen at some point. 'Total garbage' I say to the lad who has sat next to me all season as I head downstairs on the half time whistle.

'Was'na that good,' is the reply. It is probably the most in depth conversation we have had all season.

I get back to my seat just in time to witness some impromptu half time entertainment. A Stoke fan bolts from The Boothen End dressed up as Andy from Little Britain. He gambols across the penalty area and the stewards lay chase. You can almost see the stewards thinking, 'Oh no, here we go. Time to be completely humiliated in front of The Boothen End by a bloke in a wig and a pillow up his shirt.' A steward goes to trip Andy over and inevitably misses just as he makes a deft body swerve. The Stoke fans are on their feet cheering. There are a few more body swerves and for a split second it seems Andy might make it back to his seat in The Boothen End. Then a steward grabs him and the others pile on top of him. Andy is extracted from the ground to a standing ovation. Finally we get some entertainment today.

The second half is a lot better. Stoke have obviously had a rocket from Pulis and get down to business against a Wigan side that still have their minds on which exclusive resort they will be spending their holidays at this summer. With the strong wind behind Stoke, they attack The Boothen End. Pugh has replaced Cort and he blasts a thirty yard shot just over the bar.

With twenty minutes left a ball finds Fuller on the edge of the penalty area. Fuller has three Wigan defenders around him, but he twists one way and then the other. He turns and shoots. A piece of Fuller magic fires Stoke ahead and The Britannia Stadium erupts again. The goal celebration sees Abdoulaye Faye pay homage to Fuller as he mimics cleaning his boots. It is another fabulous moment. The game is put safe five minutes later. Etherington breaks free and just gets enough on a fifty fifty ball with the Wigan keeper to find Beattie unmarked at the far post. Beattie finishes it with ease. 2-0 to Stoke and it is comfortable now.

As the final minutes are played out, announcements are made to stay off the pitch at the end of the game. Last season the pitch invasion was immense. I stayed with my dad in the stand but you have to hand it to the Stoke boys. Within twenty seconds of final whistle there were ten thousand on the pitch. It has to be one of the best pitch invasions ever witnessed. That said I was disappointed the pitch was not then cleared to allow the Pulis and the players to do a lap of honour to celebrate promotion. Today I really hope the opportunity will come to show our appreciation for what has happened this season. The referee blows and nobody moves from their seats.

It will take a while for the lap of honour to be organised so I head into the concourse to see the final scores. Most things are now settled in the league, but while Stoke have been beating Wigan, there have been two incredible results in the relegation battle. Hull have got a draw away at Bolton. Newcastle, who looked home and hosed after their win against Boro, have lost at home to Fulham. Newcastle now need a result away to Villa in their last game to avoid being relegated. The feeling in the concourse is that it will be Newcastle, not Hull that will be in The Championship next season. Newcastle have been threatening total self destruction all season. Today they made good on that threat.

I head back to my seat as the lap of honour is starting. Nobody has left. Pulis leads the players, many of whom now have their kids with them, round the pitch. The PA blasts out Tina Turner. Stoke fans are more than able to show their appreciation without the help of the PA. Despite Tina's unwelcome attendance at the parade, it is still a good moment. The players appear genuinely moved, none more so than Abdoulaye Faye. It strikes me that in all the time I have supported Stoke, the bond between club, players and fans has never been stronger. It bodes well for next season and the future. The players exit and so do we. We have our usual fish and chip stop at The Riverside in Trent Vale before heading back onto the M6. It is unlikely we will return to The Potteries until August.

Arsenal Away

The last day of the season and there can be no better place to be than The Emirates Stadium on a sunny Bank Holiday weekend. Everything about this fixture had me expecting Stoke would experience a nerve wracking climax to the season. Perhaps Stoke would need points to ensure survival. Perhaps Arsenal would need points to win the league or ensure a place in The Champions League. Sometimes having such high expectations can only lead to disappointment. It happens so often in football, especially following Stoke City.

Most things are now settled in the league. Arsenal will finish fourth regardless of the result today. Stoke have a chance of finishing tenth, but it would require an unlikely scenario of winning away today and hoping Bolton beat Man City at Eastlands. Tottenham and Fulham will fight it out for seventh place, but all the other European qualification is now settled. This means that all the media attention is focussed on the bottom of the table. Boro have a mathematical chance of survival and Sunderland have a mathematical chance of relegation. Realistically though, Boro are down and one of either Hull or Newcastle will be relegated with them. Newcastle need to get a better result away to Villa than Hull get at home to Man United. Football fans everywhere will be keeping an eye on those games in the hope that Newcastle get relegated. My brother is still hoping that Hull drop after failing to close out his bet before last weekend's surprise turn around.

I meet my brother at Victoria Station. He has just arrived back from Brighton after cutting short Mackem Chris' stag weekend. We had talked earlier in the week about making

Arsenal away a huge celebration, although my suggestion to wear fancy dress had been rebuked. Having just travelled in from Reading on a train full of Arsenal fans I think my brother made the right call. We have had a late start today, so we take the tube up to Highbury & Islington straight away. We follow the crowd up Holloway Road and as we approach the stadium it suddenly feels very special.

The back streets are mobbed with thousands of Arsenal fans and the Stoke fans are making themselves heard. We turn a corner and The Emirates Stadium stands before us. I am unexpectedly blown away. As a piece of architecture it is utterly breathtaking. There is a Wembley feel to this place. I think it is the way the stadium rises out of ground and is surrounded by a raised concourse. There are now Stoke fans everywhere. They are waving flags and posing on the steps with banners for photographs. One group of Stoke fans, all in fancy dress, is huddled round a TV cameraman. I take a moment to ensure the image before me is registered and will be etched on my brain for the rest of my life. It is moments like this that make all the suffering at dumps like The County Ground and Elm Park worthwhile.

It is about 3:15pm and for once we head inside the ground early. I head straight into the arena to take a look. It is still largely empty, but it is spectacular nonetheless. What strikes me is the comfort of the place. There is loads of legroom and the seats are even padded. It is a world away from the wind swept Britannia Stadium and its cramped plastic seats, but I wouldn't swap it in a million years. Based on reputation we can expect another corporate and sterile atmosphere from the Arsenal fans this afternoon. I head back into the concourse and find my brother. The atmosphere is building up around the bars and there are plenty who have made the effort with the fancy dress.

We take our seats at 3:50pm and all the Stoke songs come out. All three thousand Stoke fans are up and singing in what is one of the nosiest away followings of the season. It might be a cliché, but a carnival atmosphere is the only word to describe it as the inflatables bounce around the away section. Whilst our relegation rivals for most of the season are nervously scrapping it out today, for us it is a day of celebration. Simonsen starts a rare game and Diao replaces an injured Etherington. Dickinson also starts today with Cort dropped. Any suspicion that Arsenal may not fancy this today is immediately wiped out. Wenger fields a strong side that is full of talent and they set about Stoke with their free flowing passing game. Arsenal are awesome and Stoke simply cannot get a look in.

Stoke are 3-0 down before twenty minutes is played. Simonson then gets injured and is substituted. It must be devastating for him. He conceded three in the first twenty minutes away to Blackburn in his last Premier League start. He is not at fault for any of the goals, but it is another disastrous start away from home for Stoke. A Beattie own goal, a van Persie penalty and a Diaby header caused the damage. The party atmosphere continues, but it is certainly dampened as thoughts of a 10-0 thrashing spring to mind. I head to the toilets on the half hour and when I return I have missed a Fuller penalty. Stoke getting back into the game seems unlikely as Arsenal are rampant. They hit the woodwork just before Stoke completely self-destruct. Delap attempts to head the ball back to Sorenson, but in doing so finds van Persie completely unmarked. 4-1 and it is game over.

We head to the concourse, but some trouble just before halftime sees the bars closed up and a hefty police presence. The day is starting to fall apart. A check on the halftime scores shows us that Villa are beating Newcastle. Newcastle have to score otherwise it doesn't matter what Hull do against Man United. My brother and I enjoy the comfort of the padded seats for the first time this afternoon. Such luxury is wasted on the Stoke support as nobody has sat down for the entire first half. The second half is a non-entity. Stoke do at least regain some composure and whilst a final score of 4-1 is bad enough, they do at least manage to avoid being totally humiliated. However, the post match statistics will show Arsenal having twenty four shots to Stoke's three, of which just one was on target. Stoke didn't even have a corner. Anybody who thinks Stoke were not completely outclassed today is kidding themselves. The only bright moment in a dismal afternoon is when the final score from the Villa game is confirmed as 1-0. Newcastle will be playing in The Championship next season.

It is hard not to leave The Emirates under a cloud. We can kid ourselves that the result today doesn't matter, but in truth it is hard to take. Sure, it has still been a good day out, but when we get back to Highbury & Islington neither of us are in the mood to carry on out on the town. The will be no champagne late into the evening as there was at the end of last season. We have had our caviar this season and tonight is a night for fish and chips. I shake my brother's hand as I get off the tube at Oxford Circus and I wonder when I will see him next. It could well be August. I arrive back in Reading at 7pm and Kate looks visibly shocked, but delighted that I am back so early. Perhaps tonight is the night to discuss my season ticket purchase for next year.

The End (or is it a New Beginning?)

We are devoted Stokies my dad, my brother and I. It runs so deep in our blood, this affliction can never be cured. The women in the family, Kate, Ellie and Daisy, my mum and my sister do not understand. They cannot cure us and will never be part of what we share through our football club. My mum plays her role in the match day routine as the provider of sandwiches, crisps and sausage rolls for our trips to The Brit. This keeps us going until we are in our spiritual home, getting our fix of pies and in my dad's case the obligatory Bovril. I can't stand the stuff myself.

My dad is a life-long fanatic who bangs on a bit about the early seventies but tends to be pessimistic. It is understandable perhaps in view of his many disappointments over sixty years of supporting Stoke City. He was at The Vic at the age of ten in 1953, when skipper Ken Thomson missed a penalty in the last match of the season against already relegated Derby County, to send Stoke down with them. Then there was Hillsborough in 1971, when a penalty in the ninety seventh minute gave Arsenal an equaliser and effectively cost Stoke a FA Cup final place. In 1972 it was Arsenal again in a semi-final replay at Goodison, when a blatantly offside goal, for which the linesman apologised afterwards, had the same effect. Given the seemingly endless misery he has endured, I think he has genuinely struggled to come to terms with the blip of success we have experienced this year. If truth be told I have little sympathy with his plight. He was fortunate enough to have been at Wembley in 1972 and also witness Alan Hudson at his peak in a Stoke shirt. I witnessed Hudson in a Stoke shirt, but only in 1985 as Stoke embarrassed themselves in the top flight in what would be their last appearance there for a generation.

So what of this season? The jury was definitely still out on Tony Pulis in our family at the start of the season. Getting Stoke promoted was nothing short of miraculous, so despite some questionable tactics I was happy to give credit where credit was due. However then going on to keep Stoke in the Premier League is an achievement in a completely different stratosphere. Sure there have been some questionable tactics and some terrible games over this season, but knowing that seventeenth place was the target and then achieving twelfth place is an over achievement by some margin. Results aside though, Pulis has really proved himself through the dignity in which he has carried himself this year. There will always be Stoke fans that don't accept him, but I for one can declare myself a convert.

So the journey ends on FA Cup Final Saturday. The lawn is finally cut and I am spending a full weekend at home as I ponder the list of household jobs that have stacked up over the last nine months. There are seventy seven days until the new season starts. I still maintain this season was a once in a lifetime experience. I have to admit I said this back in August because I thought immediate relegation was inevitable. I am so happy to be proved wrong. The anticipation ahead of Stoke's second season in The Premier League feels stronger than last year, but it will be different because the expectation of success is starting to take root. Of course there is a risk of second season syndrome, but I think Stoke is now a club more than capable of establishing themselves as a permanent fixture in The Premier League.

About the Author

Steve Mifflin was born in Cheshire, England in 1971. He attended his first Stoke City game in 1979 at The Victoria Ground where Stoke beat local rivals Derby County. From the age of seven he has been hooked and has regularly attended home and away games with his father and younger brother.

For Steve every home game is an away game as he now lives in Reading. Although the family roots run deep through Stoke-on-Trent, Steve has always had exile status from the city. The lack of a Potteries accent singles him out at The Britannia Stadium and when on the road with Stoke City.

Steve is married to Kate, a long-suffering football widow. He has two daughters Ellie and Daisy. Ellie has recently declared her allegiance to local team Reading.

Lightning Source UK Ltd.
Milton Keynes UK
24 November 2009

146646UK00001B/52/P